Personalized Reading Instruction:

New Techniques That Increase
Reading Skill and Comprehension

Personalized Reading Instruction:

New Techniques That Increase
Reading Skill and Comprehension

Walter B. Barbe and Jerry L. Abbott

Parker Publishing Company, Inc.
West Nyack, N.Y.

© 1975, *by*

PARKER PUBLISHING COMPANY, INC.

West Nyack, N. Y.

Library of Congress Cataloging in Publication Data

Barbe, Walter Burke,
    Personalized reading instruction.

    Includes bibliographical references and index.
     1. Individualized reading instruction. I. Abbott,
Jerry L.,   joint author. II. Title.
LB1050.38.B37   37.4'147   75-9861
ISBN 0-13-658104-8

Printed in the United States of America

To our families, without whose support and encouragement this book would never have been completed.

Marilyn and Fred Barbe

Sandra, Andrea and Jared Abbott

Other Works by the Authors

By Walter B. Barbe:

*Educator's Guide
to Personalized Reading Instruction*

By Jerry L. Abbott:

*Auxiliary Teacher Program:
A Complete Manual and Guide*

How This Book Will Help You Teach Reading More Effectively

Children's reading and ways in which they can become better readers continues to be of great concern. The purpose of this book is to provide an important dimension to the reading program—a personalized concern about the individual child and how he learns.

Individualization of instruction has come to be accepted as important, but the manner in which it is implemented in the classroom has varied and in many instances has been found to be either impractical or ineffective. The very definition of individualization may be confusing, for the word itself implies one-to-one teaching which may be impractical in regular classroom instruction. The personalized approach as it is presented in this book recognizes that a good reading program will use those materials and approaches which best fit the learning needs of the children in any class. But it also recognizes the need for sequential development of reading skills in order for the child to develop independence in reading.

A carefully developed, new list of reading skills is presented, beginning at the readiness level and continuing through the intermediate sixth. Arranged in a sequential, concise manner, these check lists serve as an informal diagnostic tool to indicate the skills on which the child needs help, a convenient record of each child's progress, an aid in planning skills lessons, and a guide for reporting pupil progress to parents.

As we talk with teachers from various parts of the nation we are impressed by their growing knowledge of teaching strategies. At the same time, however, there is cause for some distress with the rate at which these strategies are being implemented. Dazzled by an array of methods, gadgets, and ideas, many teachers look them over, and too often return to what is familiar.

It is a frustrating time to teach reading. At no time have we had so many programs from which to choose, yet research studies continue to indicate a lack of sufficient progress in many areas, so it is reasonable to ask what there is about this book that makes it unique. Here is the answer:

7

1) We have identified a process, that if followed, will give teachers the same if not greater sense of security than they now have in the program they are using.

2) We will provide a model for teaching reading that not only pays scrupulous attention to skill development, but also instills within each child a life-long commitment to read.

3) We include helpful processes for setting stable limits and procedures for handling students when the limits have been overridden.

4) We list practical guidelines for the conference, both individual and group, and give teachers many helpful ideas for perfecting it.

5) We describe all the sound, psychological principles that undergird this program.

6) You will learn the basis for the independent activity period and acquire realistic ideas on how to capitalize on it.

7) The key factors that influence reading levels are covered in practical detail.

8) We emphasize silent reading, the reading we do most often as adults.

9) The extraordinarily helpful Barbe Skills Check Lists will be presented for each level.

10) A detailed record-keeping system is provided that is structured enough to give the program continuity, yet flexible enough to allow for the individual differences among teachers.

11) We identify the most frequently asked questions related to personalized reading and give forthright answers on how to overcome problems.

12) We give many teacher aids in the form of IDEA Banks, charts, forms, and check lists.

As you read this book the process will clearly unfold. First you will learn about the psychological principles that form the basis of the program. Next you will be introduced to processes that will help organize the classroom for instruction. This is followed by a thorough presentation of the conferences, grouping, the independent activity period, the skills program, and record-keeping. We hope you will use many of the ideas in the beginning stages of the program. Then as you begin to feel comfortable with what you are doing, you can quickly adapt the program to fit specific needs and the needs of your students.

The chapter on Evaluating Personalized Reading is important because it details six years of action research. Reading this chapter should give you assurance that it *is* possible to leave the safe haven of the basal reader and not fear loss of achievement on standardized tests.

We end the book with a chapter entitled, "Questions Teachers Ask About Personalized Reading Instruction." The answers, based upon experience and conversations with teachers from all over the nation, will help assure you that this is a thoroughly-tested and *successful* program.

One of the unique features is that it does not cost much money. You can begin tomorrow with the materials you have. All that is needed is a description of the process, some administrative support, books and related materials from the school, and the enthusiasm to try something new. You are about to travel a new road, one from which we think you'll not return.

W.B.B.

J.L.A.

Acknowledgments

Difficult as it is to credit all of the people who have contributed to this book, we gratefully acknowledge:

all of the staff members at J. Nelson Kelly Elementary School in Grand Forks, North Dakota, whose work made it possible for us to look at this program over a period of several years and analyze its results.

elementary teachers all over the nation who have dared to leave the safe havens of the basal reader, and, in some cases, risked much.

Norma Randolph and her associates for showing us some Self Enhancing Education processes. These processes have proved to be invaluable in the teaching of personalized reading.

Contents

7. Learning to Read: The Primary Skills Program
   Reading to Learn: The Intermediate Skills Program *(Cont.)*

Mr. Simkins:

I like your period of Reading because I can read whatever I like and I don't have to get forced into reading a book I do not like. I also like it because I have my own time to read it in. I tell you I really enjoy reading and I think you learn how to read better when you read a book you like, it makes you want to read. I write all the books I read in a little booklet so I can tell everybody that can't find a good book about one of the books I read so they get interested in books. Believe me, I love to read.

From Sandra Loch

chapter one

A Model for Reading Instruction

Personalized reading instruction is a philosophy of teaching the single most important skill in the school program. Based primarily upon a philosophy which believes that every child can learn to read, and can love reading at whatever level he is able to achieve, personalized reading aims at acquiring skills and attitudes at the same time.

Little attention has been directed to the total problem of reading failures in this country. The Right to Read program, our educational moonshot of the 70's, is concerned about the children and adults who do not read well enough, but only incidentally does it speak to the total problem of reading failures: "It must be recognized . . . that for the majority who do not acquire the basic reading skills, there can also be a barrier which limits the fulfillment of their right to read. This barrier exists when the skill of reading is not accompanied by the desire to read. We fail, therefore, just as much in assuring the right to read when the desire is absent as when the skills are missing."[1] We are now far enough into the 70's to determine the effectiveness of specific Right to Read programs, and it is important to discover how many of them have found the balance between the child's right to read and his right to love reading.

The reading habits of children in our schools provide important sources of evidence concerning the long-term effects of reading instruction. An examination of library circulation statistics reveals that the amount of reading a child does decreases as he progresses through school. This decline in interest undoubtedly has much to do with the reading philosophy that comes to the surface when a school considers materials to be used in instruction.

There is evidence to show that we do not have a balance between learning how to read and learning the love of reading. Newspaper publishers are an appropriate source of information because their very existence depends upon people who not only can read but also love reading. These publishers estimate that they are selling about one-fourth as many newspapers as they should be selling. They are losing a significantly larger proportion of the readership each year . . . because society is producing non-readers in ever-increasing numbers.

Some studies report that professional people are not reading. Fader,[2] in a speech to the publishers of the nation's largest newspapers and magazines, said, "One-half of the people in this country with a bachelors degree never read another book." Roeder,[3] in a study disguised as a television survey, investigated the quantitative leisure reading habits of two groups of women—200 kindergarten through twelfth grade public school teachers and 250 women who were similar to public school teachers in several demographic and sociological respects. His conclusion was that both groups had negative attitudes toward reading as a leisure time activity. In terms of the effects upon children he says, "This evidence places even greater emphasis upon the fact that the vast majority of our children have very little contact with adults who are enthusiastic about reading and who actually pursue reading as a favored use of leisure time."

Why do teachers continue to emphasize performance at the expense of the love of reading? They do it because everything in their pre-service training tells them to do so. Recently a group of 190 elementary education majors completed an inventory in which only 17 percent listed reading as their first choice of leisure time activity. A survey of the five current methods books used in reading classes for prospective teachers revealed their major concern is teaching reading skills and not developing a love for reading. These books, used by thousands of future teachers of reading, devoted an average of 1.84 percent of the pages to reading as a lifetime skill.[4] The authors of these books obviously feel that if a child learns to read, he will continue to use the skill.

Why, then, do we continue to put our total effort into the HOW of reading? We do so because our society has been convinced that a child who can read will read. Since there is evidence that this is not true, another approach to reading is needed—one which will produce not only readers but also children who will grow into adulthood loving books and constantly enriching their lives and the lives of others by what they have found on the printed page.

Framework for Reading Instruction

It is the contention of the authors that the teacher should know every technique of teaching reading and then teach in a situation or program which allows her to use that method or technique. This, then, negates the futile exercise of deciding which is the best method of teaching material which will most effectively accomplish the goals set for any individual child or group of children reading in a school or even in a single class.

A sound method of reading instruction can be built around a three-pronged approach:

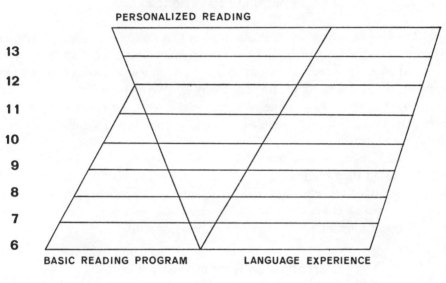

READING INSTRUCTION MODEL

PERSONALIZED READING

Figure (1-1)

A. Basic Reading Program

B. Personalized Reading Instruction

C. Language Experience

Some teachers may choose to use only the child's language or trade books in the teaching of reading, while a more structured teacher or a class which needs more structure may use basic materials. Hopefully, a class that needs to begin with a more structured program can gradually move to other components that give balance to the reading program.

Basic Reading Program

The basic program consists of one or more of the fifty developed systems that are now available. Words in color, i/t/a/, programmed reading, or one of the common basal readers are examples of systems that decode the language. There is nothing inherently wrong with any of them for some children; some children can learn to read by any of them. The key factor, however, is not the program, but the enthusiasm a teacher has for a given method.

Within the framework of the three-component model, however, the basic system is given initial emphasis and then decreased as the child progresses through school.

Language Experience

The language experience component is that part of the reading program which relies heavily upon the child's own language. It is a program that has the potential not only to teach the child how to read but also to develop within him a strong, positive self-image. Its philosophy is, "What I can think about, I can say; what I can say, I can write or someone can write for me; and what I can write, I can read." It is open-ended, success-oriented, and a highly motivating way to teach reading.

In the language experience part of the program, the children become authors, using their own works to show that we read both what others have written and what we ourselves write. The language experience approach, that component which utilizes the rich experiences children bring to school, should receive major emphasis for the child's entire school life.

Personalized Reading Instruction

Concurrently, while the basic program and language experience are being developed, the personalized component begins. The personalized program is that part of the reading program which allows children to seek, self-select, and read books at their own pace. They confer with their teacher about their books, and are grouped for skill instruction around common needs.

With a balanced emphasis on instructional methods come balanced readers. To continue giving children larger and larger doses of the basic materials without regard for the love of reading and without emphasis on individual needs is simply to add to the statistic which says that we as a nation are slowly, inexorably becoming a nation of non-readers.

Comparison of Basic Reading, Personalized Reading, and Language Experience

Most attempts to find balance in the teaching of reading have resulted in trying to prove one method superior to another. Either teaching is done from the basic materials, with some enrichment, or the basic materials are totally rejected in favor of self-selected materials. All three components, when used in the right way by an enthusiastic teacher, will be the best combination for success. If the goal of reading instruction is to produce readers who both know how to read and are committed to using the skill for life, teachers must pay attention to each of the three components as the child proceeds through his formal school experience. And if one subscribes to the theory that beginning reading instruction is "learning to read" and intermediate reading instruction is "reading to learn," the three components must be given different emphasis at various stages in the child's educational life.

The chart that follows is an attempt to show the relationship between each of the three components of a balanced reading program (Figure 1-2). It considers the important aspects of reading and shows how the weakness of one can be a strength of another. For instance, basic systems have for a long time been known for their careful attention to sequence and the help for the teacher in the manuals. But they also have a very carefully controlled vocabulary and are of limited interest to a large number of children. Careful blending by an understanding of the strengths of each component has the potential of giving each child the best possible instruction in reading.

Summary

Personalized reading instruction is a philosophy of teaching as well as an approach to classroom organization. Based upon the concept of each child's need for seeking, self-selection, and self-pacing, the personalized program is one part of a total program which might include the basic program, personalized instruction and a language experience approach. A comparison of each of these is given in this chapter.

FOOTNOTES

[1]James E. Allen, "The Right to Read," Speech given at the National Association of State School Boards of Education, Los Angeles, California, September 23, 1969, p. 3.

[2]Daniel Fader, "What Will a Child Read?", Speech given at a national meeting of newspaper and magazine publishers, Miami, Florida, 1966.

[3]Harold H. Roeder, "A Comparison Between the Leisure Reading Habits of Female Teachers and Other Women of the Same Social Status," *The Psychology of Reading Behavior*, (Eighteenth Yearbook), G.B. Schick, ed. (Milwaukee, Wisconsin: National Reading Conference, Inc., 1969), p. 60.

[4]John W. Stewig, "Instructional Strategies," *Elementary English*, Vol. 50, No. 6, September 1973, p. 922.

COMPARISON OF BASIC READING, PERSONALIZED READING, AND LANGUAGE EXPERIENCE

	BASIC PROGRAM	PERSONALIZED READING	LANGUAGE EXPERIENCE
Overall Goal of Instruction:	Children will read as adults if they know how Develop good oral readers	"How to read" must be balanced with the development of a "love for reading."—Sustain silent reading as early as possible	Exciting children about their own thoughts and experiences will springboard them into both knowing "How to read" and to "love reading"
Role of the Teacher:	Usually works with one of several groups or supervises a paper-pencil activity in the independent work period	Spends half or more time conferencing with children—When not conferencing can be found teaching need groups, completing student records, supervising a project in book sharing, or helping at a center of interest	Much time devoted to reassuring the child of his vast knowledge and using each child's experience as a unique resource in helping other children develop their language
Motivation:	Manual suggests techniques to use to motivate the child to read the story	Motivation comes from within as the result of reading self-selected materials and sharing them with his teacher and friends	Motivation comes from the power of the child's own language
Selection of Stories:	Carefully selected by authors and graded according to vocabulary difficulty	Selected by students from a broad range of interest and difficulty level	Stories are produced by students from a broad range of experiences

Reading Level:		
Reads at the level of the group Some provision for development of his own interests	Reads at his own level and what is of interest to him	Reads what he has written or what someone has written for him
Vocabulary Control:		
Controlled by the authors— Each succeeding story introduces more difficult vocabulary	Vocabulary development is open-ended	A power vocabulary develops out of the child's own experience
Questioning:		
Often, but not always, the teacher relies upon convergent questions (Ex.: Find the line . . . How many kittens were running . . . ?)	Heavy emphasis upon divergence (Ex.: What do you think . . . ? Has that ever happened to you . . . ? How did you feel . . . ?)	The uniqueness of each child's experiences brings out the ultimate in open-minded questioning
Grouping:		
Groups decided early in the year and usually for the entire year—When the child is ready for more difficult work, the next group has also moved onto more difficult work, leaving him in the same group	Groups are very fluid, forming and dissolving as soon as common needs are met Conference gives hints to grouping	Heavy use of whole class grouping, small groups, and individual conferencing, all of which are to get ideas flowing

BASIC PROGRAM	PERSONALIZED READING	LANGUAGE EXPERIENCE
Record-Keeping:		
Record-keeping systems usually accompany basic series—Most emphasize books read, end of book tests, and the date completed—Records kept in child's cumulative folder in school office	Because sequential development of skills is the total responsibility of the teacher, a very careful accounting of skills is kept—skills check lists, charts, and forms of various kinds are used and given to each succeeding teacher for use the following year	Skill instruction taught on the basis of need—Skills come out of the child's experiences and then used to reinforce skill teaching from basic system—Pupil accounting similar to that of personalized reading
Skills:		
Well-developed teacher's manuals include a sequentially developed skills program	Teacher uses one of several well developed skills check lists available from several sources	Same as for personalized reading
Skills usually taught to quite large groups of students, before reading, and followed by reteaching to those that did not comprehend	(See Barbe Skills Check List) The philosophy of skill instruction is quite different from most basic series—Basic program says, "You learn the skills and then read"; the personalized program says, "You learn to read by reading"—The skills that are not known are then taught—Much emphasis of skill work takes place in handwriting and spelling, thereby keeping reading somewhat free from too much analysis and synthesis of words	
Decoding precedes encoding		Encoding precedes decoding or is concurrently developed

Figure (1-2)

26

chapter two

Organizing a Classroom for Personalized Reading Instruction

Organizing the classroom for personalized reading instruction is difficult for some teachers because it requires behavior that might be quite foreign to them. Typically, teachers have placed themselves in the role of authoritarian in the classroom. They are the model to imitate and with which to identify, (with no feedback) the influencer of behavior, attitudes, and values, and offer instruction in rather explicit terms.[1]

Teachers of personalized reading must take another approach. They must move from the authoritarian role to one of authority, to a role that utilizes children as a unique resource of their own feelings and perceptions. The shift from authoritarian behavior to that of authority can best be described by the chart, Figure (2-1), that follows.

The traditional classroom organization for reading instruction is that of three groups under the direct guidance of the teacher, with nearly all program decisions made by the teacher. Teachers of personalized reading spend much more time with children on a one-to-one basis. The teacher is no longer a controller but a facilitator of learning. The emphasis is shifted from the instruction of the group to the instruction of the individual. This one-to-one basis of instruction should immediately alert teachers to the need for children to make many program decisions on their own. If this provision for student involvement is not made, there is danger that personalized reading will never fulfill its intended purposes.

Teacher Behavior

Typical Teacher Behavior	New Behavior Required for PRI
A. Director of Learning Experience	A. Facilitator of Learning Experience
B. Emphasizes Whole Group Instruction with Some Small Group Work	B. Fluid Groupings That Meet Only for as Long as There Is a Need
C. Student Movement Is Teacher Directed	C. Freedom to Move Within Stable Limits
D. Pupil Options Selected by Teacher	D. Options Selected by Teacher in Cooperation with the Child
E. Teacher Describes Appropriate Behavior	E. The Activity Determines the Behavior
F. Scrupulous Attention to Housekeeping	F. Housekeeping Not a Constant Source of Frustration and Concern
G. Teacher Sets Stable Limits	G. Teacher Using Children as a Unique Resource Set Stable Limits

Figure (2-1)

Beginning a Personalized Reading Program

The classroom teacher must do as much preplanning as possible and should read everything readily available on the subject of personalized reading. She may visit with others who are using the personalized method and implement hers a little at a time. And whenever initiating anything in a school, it is wise to have others involved. When several are involved in the same innovation, there is a solid base for sharing and expanding the program.

The teacher should look at the program she is using and ask herself some questions: "Do I have one basal or multi-basals?" "Do I read one story after another, or do I sometimes read them out of sequence?" "When Thanksgiving comes, do I feel free to go to the back of the book and read a story about Pilgrims or must I read the story that comes next?" If a teacher is now flexible with the materials she uses, she has the prerequisite skills to move into the personalized reading program.

There are many decisions to make, such as when to begin and with whom (the whole class? the gifted children? the slowest readers?). These are decisions that the teacher must make, and will depend to a large degree upon how she perceives children and the goals of reading. However, the literature is full of rationale concerning which children should be instructed with the personalized method. Some make a good case for the retarded reader because he is the child for whom basal materials are not appropriate. Another will say the same thing for the gifted reader. Still others argue that all children, from the beginning, should be in personalized reading. The teacher must try to determine what is right for her and her pupils and begin.

Using Children as Resources

The wise teacher uses her students as unique resources by continually calling for feedback from them. Some teachers use the class meeting technique as described by Glasser and associates. Others simply ask the children on a regular basis: "What about the lesson gave you a good feeling?" and "What about the lesson gave you concern?" Whatever method is used, it is imperative that children's perceptions be considered, or the program will never realize its full potential.

When children are questioned for their opinion, it is important that the teacher steer away from the defensive. If a child gives his honest perception of reading class and it does not agree with hers, the teacher must not indicate displeasure. Doing so will endanger the effectiveness of the feedback technique. Each child's input should be taken in as nonjudgmental a way as possible to assure the children that the teacher is genuinely interested in improving the reading program. It will take time and effort to get from the children the commitment necessary to make the personalized reading approach function properly.

The Personalized Reading Instruction Model

It is imperative that teachers choosing to work in this way have an overall concept of what personalized reading attempts to accomplish. The model presented below should help in that regard. There are various components around which personalized reading is based, and a thorough understanding of each is necessary for a successful program.

A chart or transparency of the personalized reading model can be made and shown to the children. The teacher should identify each part of the new program and involve the children as deeply as possible in its organization and implementation. Like a torpedo moving toward its target and the computer correcting for error, the teacher should continue to ask the children, "What gives you a good feeling?" and "What gives you concern?"

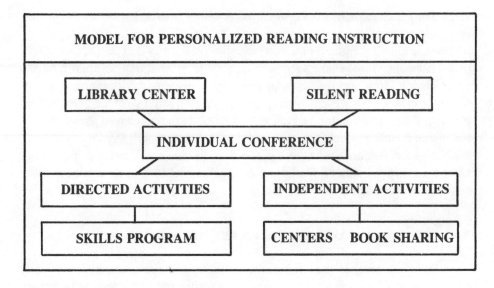

Figure (2-2)

The Library Center

The library center and its construction are important to personalized reading instruction because these elements are the beginning of a move away from the three-group approach and the paper-pencil work that is so much a part of many reading programs. For many classrooms, the library center may be the first indication that there is more to reading than "how to."

Although there are a number of ways the teacher can begin arousing the children's interest in a library center, the opening conversation could go like this: "Boys and girls, I am concerned about the way our room is organized. There doesn't seem to be enough space for all of us to feel comfortable, and I often hear you complain about too much noise. I wonder if we could talk about this?" With that kind of opening, the teacher can be assured that ideas will come fast and furiously. In fact, she may get many more than can be implemented. Nevertheless, it is this kind of cooperative endeavor and involvement that will make the program a success.

The library center should enjoy an honored place in the classroom. Deciding where the center is to be located, its rules of operation, and keeping it stocked should be a total class decision, with the teacher acting as helper and facilitator.

The library center should be out-of-bounds as a place to do anything except examine and read books. Jeannette Veatch says it best: "The book center is not a place of instruction—in the sense that the teacher directly teaches there—it is a place for browsing, for looking over books, for selecting those desired, for quiet contemplation of the bountiful world of books."[2]

The first thing that will make the center attractive is a large rug or carpet.

It can be arranged close to some shelves in such a way as to make it both a storage area for books and a divider to assure some privacy. The addition of lamps, sofas, stuffed chairs, and pillows will further attract children to this area.

Books, newspapers, and magazines should be displayed in the most attractive way possible. Books should never be arranged end to end with only the bindings showing. Instead, they can be displayed in unusual ways, with the book jackets remaining on until they fall off from wear. The teacher may go to the neighborhood bookstore and ask the proprietor to loan some paperback racks. She may also visit the manager of every supermarket and department store in the surrounding area and ask them to save display racks. These make wonderful, magnetic displays since they usually have the imprints of some of the children's favorite storybook characters. While there, the teacher should be sure to find out when there will be a special sale of paperbacks, Classic comics, etc.

Other methods of display which have been used with success are fun to do and are creative for the teacher and children alike. For example, the group can hang a series of long dowels from the beams or from the roof constructed over the center. Books, paperbacks, magazines, newspapers, and comics can be displayed over the dowels. A large metal ring can be suspended from the ceiling, with a number of short, colorful strings fastened from the ring and a clothespin placed on the end of each string. This is especially good for displaying some of the most important books in the center, including those made by the children in the language experience portion of the program. It is also possible to display the books in such a way that matches them with a booksharing project. For instance, the book jacket can be taken off and replaced with one a child has made. This will entice other children to read the book.

A listening station may be set up near the library center and stocked with records and tapes that accompany many of the books on display. The teacher might find it worthwhile to write to an author and ask him to make a tape regarding his book or books and then display his books with the tape and an invitation both to listen to the tape and to check out the book. Charts which bring to attention unusual things about a book or books may also be used. (For example, "Can you find the book that . . . ?," "Did you know that . . . ?," and "There is a book on the pile that . . . !)

The teacher should be aware of everything that might deter children from using the library center. A conscious effort should be made to avoid this. For instance, the teacher should not require that all books be read in school, discourage checkout during the weekends or holidays, or allow the child to check out only one book at a time. Imposing a rigid set of rules for either the library center or the central library, such as requiring that children go to the central library only when they are accompanied by the teacher and the rest of the class, or imposing fines for overdue books, will tend to decrease enthusiasm. Using reading as a system of rewards and punishments (e.g., "you have finished your work, so you can read") is not advisable. The presence of an "easy book" section either in the classroom center or the library should also be avoided. The teacher should never be overly critical of children's choices when they are within reasonable limits and should not become too concerned if a child decides that he doesn't like the book he is reading and wants another.

An attractive library helps to encourage self-selection, but there will be times when the classroom teacher will need to give self-selection a little push. The teacher may encourage the principal to show an interest in books. He should see children reading, and they should see him reading. When new shipments of books arrive, the teacher may ask the principal to announce it to the whole school over the intercom or through a news bulletin. She may also ask the principal to bring books from the book clubs to the classroom as soon as they arrive. The teacher should stop what she is doing and, together with the principal and students, form a circle to discuss the new arrivals. Or, new books may be displayed in the central library so the children can stop by and examine them before they go home, allowing them to check them out as soon as they are properly catalogued.

The teacher should always try to have a partially finished book on the desk. Occasionally, when appropriate, it can be used as a conversation piece, with the teacher talking with the children about what she is reading.

Invitations may be extended to teachers, principals, hostesses, custodians, bus drivers, or parents to come before the class and try to "sell" the latest book they have read. The manager of a bookstore may also come to the classroom and talk about books that seem to be selling best. Or, local authors may be invited to the classroom to talk about their books or experiences they have had in gathering information for a book or in writing a book.

Silent Reading

Personalized reading instruction places heavy emphasis upon silent reading because most of our reading as adults is silent. Therefore, one of the tasks of the teacher is to sustain silent reading for as long as possible in each child.

Once the idea of the reading center has been firmly established, the teacher should talk with children about silent reading. She should tell them that one of the major goals of this part of the program is to find out how long they can sustain themselves silently and that they are working to increase the length of time that they can read silently from a self-selected book. Some children have trouble internalizing the fact that their chosen book is their reading book.

The teacher may ask them to name a favorite book and then say, "If this is the book you choose to read, this will take the place of your present reader."

Keeping in mind the overall goal of involvement, the teacher should take some time to discuss this aspect of the program. The children will be interested in where they can read in the room, what they do when they need help, what they do when they have finished the book, and so on. Once these guidelines have been established, it is wise to introduce the "plan for the day" concept. This plan will contain those things the teacher feels need to be accomplished and some options that each child may choose. It should be read each day before beginning the reading class. The plan for the day is a good place to indicate which children will conference with the teacher while the rest are reading silently from a book they have chosen. The plan for the day should also help to decrease the number of interruptions that would hinder the conferences and the silent reading period.

Once the child has selected his book and the teacher has signaled the silent reading period, the child should feel free to read in as comfortable a setting as possible. Some children who are particularly sensitive to stimuli can be found reading in a study carell, inside a container of some kind, or under the teacher's desk. Others may choose to read at their desk, on the floor, or in the cloakroom. The place is not so important as the fact that the child is reading a book that interests him.

A child should read until he "reads himself out," meaning that he reads until he can no longer sustain himself. If the book is of very high interest, he might sustain himself for an hour or more. Probably 20 to 40 minutes would be the range of time for most intermediate children.

During silent reading there will be children who need help. Because the teacher is holding conferences with other children, she cannot be interrupted by those in immediate need. There are several things the teacher can do: (1) she can use the children with whom she conferenced the preceding day as word helpers; (2) she can make charts as aids to unlocking words; or (3) she can utilize other personnel in the classroom, like teacher aides, student teachers, or parent aides. The classroom teacher cannot operate the program alone, working in the same way as before. Whenever the teacher finds things that need repeating, she should make a chart and call each child's attention to it to help economize time. The teacher must also use the children as a unique resource. Once they are aware of the reasons behind using them as aides, they will be of great help.

There is simply no reason for not using resources in the community. It is full of people waiting to be asked to help. If the teacher is fortunate to be in a university community, the potential for help is unlimited. If not, she may simply call a meeting of parents and explain any problems. She can be sure that some of them will offer their assistance.

Uninterrupted Sustained Silent Reading

Most programs of personalized reading begin each day with a short discussion about the reading period. This is followed by whole-class silent reading
and the teacher having conferences with selected children. An alternative to
this procedure on one or two days per week is Uninterrupted Sustained Silent
Reading. This method was first used by Dr. Lyman Hunt as a way to focus
upon the importance of silent reading.

It is Hunt's contention that many of the nation's children are "over-
taught" and "under-practiced" through our emphasis on oral reading. In giving rationale for the Uninterrupted Sustained Silent Reading technique he says,
"Basic to this concept is the consideration that silent reading is far more
significant than is oral reading. Basic to this concept is the belief that contex-
tual reading is of greater importance than are skills of recognition at the word
letter level. Basic to the concept is that the greatest reading skill to be achieved
is that of sustaining silent reading over long stretches of print without interrup-
tion and without breaks. Uninterrupted Sustained Silent Reading cannot be
achieved unless the reader has the facility to keep his mind on and flowing with
ideas."[3]

Too many of our reading programs are dominated by oral reading. Many
slow readers are embarrassed by the teacher's insistence upon their reaching a
high level of fluency in oral reading when for them it may be an impossibility.
What they need, along with skill instruction, is initial emphasis placed upon
silent reading. Then after this opportunity to interact privately with books
without fear of failure, they can attain fluency in oral reading.

In summarizing the child's responsibilities during Uninterrupted Sustained Silent Reading, Dr. Hunt says, "Each child realized that doing well
means: (1) accomplishing as much silent reading as possible during the reading
period; (2) keeping one's mind on the ideas; (3) responding more powerfully to
high potency words and sentences; and (4) giving less attention to ideas of
lesser importance."[4]

Dr. Robert McCracken also uses this technique and calls it Sustained
Silent Reading. He lists six rules that must be followed rigidly, especially in
the beginning weeks of the program:

1. Each child must read silently with no interruptions.
2. The teacher reads silently.
3. Each child selects his own reading material.
4. A timer is used to increase sustaining time.
5. There are absolutely no reports of any kind.
6. The program is begun with the whole class.[5]

In orienting the children to this technique it might be well for the teacher to talk with them in small groups prior to its initiation. She should answer any questions they have and role-play any or all of the processes.

The teacher should explain to the children that the purpose of this experiment is to see how long they can sustain themselves in a self-selected book and that the object of the experiment is to try to increase this time. It is best to use a timer and not a clock for this method because the children tend to become clock-watchers. An hour glass, an alarm clock, or a commercial cooking timer are all very good. The teacher might begin with the timer set for five minutes. Hopefully, a period of an hour or more will be reached with intermediate children after a few weeks.

The younger the children are the more help they will need with selection of reading materials. For very young children, the teacher might sit in a circle with a large number of appropriate, well-illustrated books. She may pull one from the pile and talk about it, repeating the process with the rest of the books. Then the children may be asked to select a book. When the teacher starts the timer, the children are to do their best at finding ideas through silent reading. They should not trade books, nor should they talk to anyone. The teacher will be reading, too, and they must understand that she is not to be disturbed. After three or four minutes, the teacher should stop, tell the children how proud she is of their silent reading, and let them know that the next day their time period will be increased. With older children, however, it is not necessary to have so many preliminaries. If already engaged in a program of personalized reading, they will know most of the rationale behind trying to sustain silent reading.

The teacher should assure the children that the objective of sustained silent reading is not any kind of follow-up testing other than some very general whole-class questioning. There are no reports to be made, and the pupils do not have to share the book in any way—unless, of course, they decide to bring that book into the personalized reading period and it becomes a book they bring to the conference.

The whole class is involved for two reasons: (1) the teacher reads, too, and therefore, is not available to help anyone; and (2) when the main object is sustaining silent reading over long stretches of print and looking for ideas, with no follow-up, there is no limit to the numbers of children who can participate.

Anytime the teacher does something with the class it is wise to have a short period for evaluation. Dr. Hunt has identified the following general questions that could be used periodically as a way to stimulate thinking about the books:

1. Did you have a good reading period today? Did you read well? Did you get a lot done?
2. Did you read better today than yesterday?

3. Were you able to concentrate today on your silent reading?
4. Did the ideas in the book hold your attention? Did you have the feeling of moving right along with them?
5. Did you have the feeling of wanting to go ahead faster to find out what happened? Were you constantly moving ahead to get the next good part?
6. Was it hard to keep your mind on your reading?
7. Were you bothered by others or outside noises?
8. Could you keep the ideas in your book straight in your mind?
9. Did you get mixed up in any place? Did you have to go back and straighten yourself out?
10. Were there words you did not know? How did you figure them out?
11. What did you do when you got to the good points? Did you read faster or slower?
12. Were you always counting to see how many pages you had left to go? Were you wondering how long it would take you to finish?
13. Were you hoping that the book would go on and on—that it would really not end?[6]

As the program matures, and the children begin to sustain themselves for more than 30 minutes, the teacher can begin to relax some of the rules. Of course, the children should be taught never to violate the rules of no interruptions, self-selection, and teacher participation. The timer may perhaps be eliminated after a few weeks and more sharing elicited. When reading is good, sharing cannot be prevented, and the children will no doubt overwhelm the teacher with ideas they have gleaned from their reading. The teacher should elicit all the ideas possible, and before long this technique will have become an integral part of the personalized reading program.

If she has any concerns about how the children are perceiving the program, the teacher may simply ask, "What about Uninterrupted Silent Reading gives you a good feeling?" and "What about it gives you concern?"

Individual Conference

The individual conference is the central component of the personalized reading program. The children must be totally aware of its significance and method of operation. The teacher should take the time to explain to her pupils that some of the group work consumes almost all of the reading period and that a one-to-one conference would perhaps be a better way of teaching reading. The teacher may also talk about the guidance function of the conference or the individual diagnosis that takes place during the conference.

Once again, the main point to remember is student involvement. The teacher should not try to impose any of her plans on the children. Even though she may have an answer for every question asked, the teacher should not offer them all at once. It is important to get every perception possible from the children. As problems arise, the teacher may offer her suggestions as possible solutions.

The individual conference is one of the most crucial parts of the entire program. Everything that comes before it leads to it, and everything that comes after it is a direct result of it. A more detailed study of the individual conference is presented in Chapter four.

Directed Group Activities

In this part of the program it is important that children understand the value of learning reading skills. Talk about the traditional way in which skills are presented. Ask them what about it makes them feel good and what about it gives them concern. They will no doubt bring up a concern about too much paper-pencil work, relearning skills they already know, and the problems of transferring skills from reading class to other situations. Discuss ways in which this is different.

Independent Activities

Ask the children if they prefer doing things that have a prescribed answer, or if they like to do things that have many answers. They will no doubt choose the latter. Children love divergence.

Using the chart or transparency, talk about centers of interest and book-sharing as techniques for open-endedness. After each book is read the child should decide whether or not he has enough interest in it to share it with other children or his teacher. If so, he chooses one of many book-sharing ideas available.

Talk with the children about centers of interest and why they are an important part of the personalized program. Discuss their potential for divergence and how easily they can correlate with books that have been read.

Now review the entire process with the children. Make sure they understand the reasons for each component of the program. If two or three children are still confused, group them and go over the plan once again.

Stable Limits

Personalized reading requires teacher behavior different from that required by the basal program. Emphasis will change from large groups to small groups and individual conferences, from teacher selection to self-selection, and from the teacher being in charge to the children being in charge of themselves . . . and hopefully, each other.

Educators for years have been identifying processes to help children and adults take charge of themselves. Self-Enhancing Education is one group which has done much to identify processes that help children become self-directed enough to participate successfully in programs like personalized reading instruction. Following is an example of how one of their processes might be used:

> Boys and girls, before we begin this program, I think we need to talk about stable limits. Stable limits are like boundaries or fences within which we can feel free to function without having to wonder and test. Hopefully, these boundaries will be confining enough so we can be responsible persons, yet large enough to allow us to express fully our creativity. We need the security of stable limits so we don't waste a lot of our time testing. If you constantly test, I will respond with a lot of admonishment and command. That doesn't feel very good to me, and I am sure it won't feel very good to you.

As the teacher talks with the children about stable limits, it shouldn't be very long before someone discovers one of the most basic principles of stable limits: *Allow the activity to determine the behavior*. Children are participating in many different kinds of activities when they self-select a book, read it silently, conference with the teacher about its contents, go to a skills lesson because of trouble with the main idea in a paragraph, make a book-sharing project, or play an educational game at a center of interest. The children should not be required to behave the same way for all of these activities. The activity must determine the behavior, and the teacher must reinforce this principle again and again. If the activity is making a book-sharing project, it might be very appropriate to make noise. If most of the class is reading silently, the children have a responsibility to each other to be quiet.

Applying Process to Self-Management

The following Self-Enhancing Education process will be helpful in providing self-management in the classroom and freeing the teacher to work with individuals while the rest of the class is working in self-selected materials:

1. Carefully describe or co-plan the activity or routine.
2. Elicit the social behaviors required to make it through the activity.
3. Call for the adult (the call to be in charge of self).
4. Do not pitchfork (Overchecking).
5. Set a time limit and come back before the deadline to offer help.[7]

Activities are constantly changing throughout the day. The teacher does not have time, nor would it be productive, to stop class continually and talk about the social behaviors that are required for each new activity. Therefore, a process is needed that, once learned, has utility for the entire school day.

Once the children understand that the program involves self-selection, silent reading, conferencing, skill work, flexible groupings, book-sharing, and centers of interest, the teacher can ask her pupils to describe the activities discussed. They should be able to describe them as the first step of the personalized reading program.

After all of the activities have been carefully described, the teacher reminds the children once again of the new law of behavior: *Allow the activity to determine the behavior.* She should then ask, "What kinds of behavior will it take to make it through all of the activities we have described?" With a little help on the part of the teacher, the list could go something like this:

1. Plan for the day:
   The beginning minutes of the day are the most important, for it is here that the teacher presents the plan. I carefully read what I must do and what is optional for me to do. I will listen attentively when the teacher is working through the plan.

2. Selection of a book:
   If the book I am reading is too difficult, too easy, or completed, I will select another book. I will not make excessive noise as I go to the library center. If there are more than five children at the center, I will wait until someone leaves.

3. Read yourself out:
   This is the quietest time of the day. I will show my respect for others by not making any noise during this time.

4. Responsibilities before the conference:
   A. If I had a conference yesterday, it means that I now have one or more jobs to carry out. If I am a word helper, I will respond to anyone who asks for help. If I am the distributor of supplies and equipment, I will make sure it is done in such a way as not to disturb the teacher or the child in conference.
   B. If I am to have a conference today, I will watch to make sure I am there when it is my turn.

5. Waiting chair:
   As soon as the person ahead of me leaves the waiting chair and goes to his conference, I will proceed to the waiting chair with a minimum of noise.

6. Conference:
   A. I will not do anything to disturb anyone who is having a conference.
   B. I will go to the conference as soon as the person ahead of me finishes.
   C. I will carry out any jobs I have so the teacher can devote her time to conferencing with other children.
   D. I will try to the best of my ability to carry out all assignments that I get during the conference.

7. Skills class:
   Sometimes the skills class is taught by a teacher aide, a student aide, or a parent volunteer. I will show the same respect for them as I do for my regular teacher.

8. Independent Acitivity:
   A. As soon as my skills work is completed, I will go to an independent activity. (Book-Sharing, Centers)
   B. If the independent activity is disturbing to others, I will signal the teacher that I am leaving the room.

Once the activities have been carefully described and the social behaviors necessary to carry out these activities have been elicited, the teacher must call for each child to be in charge of self. This calls for a possible value change on the part of the teacher. If she believes that children respond best to admonishment and command, the self-management plan will be very difficult to carry out. If, on the other hand, the teacher feels that all children have the potential to be in charge of self, the task will be much easier.

There is something very powerful in asking people to take charge of themselves. Most children should respond positively if asked to do so. Of course, there will be times when the children have a difficult time controlling themselves. If some children are having a great amount of difficulty concentrating on or doing a task, the teacher can either take them away from the task for a while or group them and offer help. Also, the teacher may give a child a task, only to find him doing something else. It will be tempting to shout a reprimand across the room, but the teacher should let the child do what he is doing. Then prior to the predetermined deadline, she should ask him what she can do to help. It is surprising how many tasks will be completed in the last moments before the deadline.

Slowly the teacher will see her role change from the commander to the facilitator. Interruptions at conference time will diminish, and the children will manage themselves with little teacher intervention.

If the teacher sees that the plan is breaking down, she should call a class meeting and talk about what has happened. If only four or five children are having trouble they should be dealt with in a group. If behavior makes the teacher angry, they should be told exactly that. The teacher must remember, however, that anger and frustration is directed not at the children, but at their behavior. When the self-management process begins to break down, the teacher must not hesitate to say, "I can see by your behavior that you want me to take charge of you for a while. I will do that until you are back in charge of yourselves."

Overriding Stable Limits

The process that has been described has universal application in setting limits and helping people of all ages manage themselves. Yet some children have continued trouble managing themselves. The following Self-Enhancing Education process will be helpful to the teacher when children override the stable limits they have set for themselves:

1. Read the infringement as an unclear message, not as defiance of authority.
2. Present your puzzlement, showing ownership of the feeling.
3. Invite clarification by using reflective listening.*
4. Honor the feelings of the sender; state where you stand, being as nonjudgmental as possible, and invite proposed solutions.
5. Clarify that what is needed is responsibility, not punishment for punishment's sake.[8]

A very common problem in personalized reading is that of trying to have conferences without being interrupted. Interruptions are annoying and diminish the thrust of the conference. The following example of conversation is based on

---

*In our traditional culture, we have not learned to listen effectively to one who is sending a message. We have not learned to listen to the perception and feelings of another person, and have not responded to him in such a way that he knows we have heard him. We traditionally judge his perception or feeling as right or wrong, good or bad, and then agree or disagree. What we have really done is to leave out a very important step in the communication process. This omission blunts two-way communication. We can find many illustrations around us of this blunting communication—divorce, generation gap, alienation of youth, rebellion, and unhappy individuals.

To hear adequately the message of the sender, the receiver has to hold in abeyance or suspend his own feelings and perceptions. Then he can feed back the message to check his accuracy and to assure the listener that he has heard correctly. (A serious inquiry into reflective listening can be found in *Self-Enhancing Education: A Training Manual*, Randolph, Howe, and Achterman (Santa Clara, California, SEE, Inc., 1971.)

the process earlier identified and can be used as a guideline for dealing with a child who is continually interrupting during conferences:

Teacher: "John, do you remember when we talked about student behavior during conferences?"

John: "Yes."

Teacher: "Well, for the last three days you have interrupted me during conference time, and it is very annoying both to me and to the child with whom I am having the conference. I am wondering what this behavior is telling me. Can you take charge of yourself, or are you asking me to take charge of you?"

John: "I forgot."

Teacher: "You didn't remember your responsibilities?"

John: "I forgot the assignments."

Teacher: "You didn't remember the plan for the day. I thought I had gone over it rather thoroughly each day before reading class."

John: "It wasn't your fault. It was Phil."

Teacher: "Phil is causing you to interrupt me while I am having conferences?"

John: "No. Phil and I live next door to each other. The other night we didn't come in until 11:00 p.m. Our folks won't let us go out after supper for a whole week."

Teacher: "So you have been using this time to catch up on things you ordinarily do after supper?"

John: "I guess so."

Teacher: "I know you guys are friends, and I can understand that you need some time to talk things over now that you are grounded, but I can't let you continue to interrupt me during conferences. I wonder what we can do about this."

John: "You can make us stay after school."

Teacher: "That would be one way to go. Can you think of another?"

John: "You could move us."

Teacher: "Yes."

John: "Or maybe we could listen better during morning planning time and save what we have to say until break time."

Teacher: "I don't think I would feel very good about punishing you. I kind of like the idea of trying to save what you have to say to each other until break time. Why don't you talk that over with Phil and try it for a few days? Let's talk again in about three days and see how your plan is working. Is this OK with you, John?"

John: "Yes."

The steps of this process are universal in application. Once the steps are internalized, the process can be used over and over to achieve satisfactory solutions to classroom behavior problems.

Role-Playing

Up to this point we have described personalized reading, unlocked processes for implementing it, and described a plan for successful implementation. Role-playing is another technique that has the potential to bring all of these processes into focus.

Role-playing, or the acting out of situations in a friendly setting, has the potential to:

1. Develop instant cohesion between groups of people.
2. Firmly implant process in the minds of students.
3. Help class members develop feeling for each other.
4. Capitalize on play, a powerful learning technique.
5. Help anticipate problems.
6. Build confidence.
7. Build awareness.
8. Help us not to take ourselves too seriously.

After the whole group has had some experience with role-playing, it can be used as a device to help those children who are having difficulty with a certain aspect of personalized reading instruction. The following situations may be role-played in order that they might be better internalized by the children:

1. Rules for the library center.
2. How to select a book.
3. Silent reading in various parts of the room.
4. A conference with the teacher.
5. The principal interrupting the teacher while she is in a conference.
6. A child who doesn't know a word.
7. How to keep records.
8. What to do when you need to go to the bathroom, the library, the office.
9. Playing a game at a center of interest.
10. Practicing a play when the remainder of the class is carrying out other parts of personalized reading.

11. Selecting the book of the week.
12. Making a book-sharing project.
13. A parent who is concerned because her child is not reading out of the basal reader.
14. Clean-up at the end of the period.
15. Small group discussion about a skills lesson, a book read, or a play you have just seen.
16. The entire personalized reading process.

Children are hams. It will not be difficult to invite them into role-playing situations. If the teacher does encounter difficulty, she may ask the children to role-play with a partner and then ask for volunteers, or she may role-play with a student who wishes to role play with her. She should never force someone to role play if he does not feel comfortable with it.

It is important to take some time to talk about individual and group responsibilities during role-playing. If two children are making an honest effort to role-play a situation, each member of the class has a responsibility to support them and not make fun of them. Children must be impressed with the fact that there are no winners and losers in role-playing. Therefore, they should not make inputs that are difficult and so far from reality that it makes answering difficult. Neither should they break out of role until the situation has been acted out to its completion.

Role-playing is one of the most beneficial techniques that can be used to insure the success of this program. Once the process has been captured, the teacher and class should take some time to evaluate it. It won't be long before these processes will make valuable impact upon the personalized reading program.

Summary

This chapter has been an attempt to briefly introduce the reader to each component of the personalized program and apply the process of self-management to personalized reading.

We continue to hear teachers say that this program sounds good but they are afraid of what might happen to the discipline in their classroom. We think this problem can be solved if teachers will apply these principles.

The literature abounds in debate about how classrooms should be organized for instruction. It ranges from tight structure to very "open" kinds of arrangements. We think the process that has been identified represents the best of both.

Classroom Organization IDEA Bank

1. If checkout of books is a problem, give each child a library card. When he checks out a book, he puts his card with the book card in a box. This will have the double effect of letting the children know who has what book and stimulating them to want to read a book because someone else is reading it.

2. When children do not respond to freedom at the library center, make a set of cards and number them one to five. Only five children can use the center at one time. As soon as one child leaves the center he places the card on a table. This is a signal that another child can use the center.

3. Use one of the following techniques with staff members to internalize the purposes of personalized reading:
   A. Discuss: Can all teachers learn the required behaviors for success in personalized reading?
   B. Discuss: Can children learn to be responsible for self?
   C. Visit a classroom where personalized reading is being used. Report to the staff.
   D. Try out one of the Self-Enhancing Education processes in the classroom. Report to the staff on its success or failure.
   E. Ask each staff member to bring information to the staff meeting that either supports or discourages the use of personalized reading. Discuss.
   F. Ask a teacher using personalized reading to bring some of her students to a staff meeting. Discuss the advantages and disadvantages.

4. Have a meeting with your children and ask them the following questions: "What about reading gives you a good feeling?" "What about reading gives you concern?" This could be made more interesting by having each staff member bring his list to a staff meeting. It would be a very accurate way of determining directions in reading.

5. Using the following procedure, role-play the entire process to allow the children to internalize personalized reading:
   A. Put a sample "Plan for the Day" on the chalkboard. It could include those who will conference, those skills that need to be accomplished, and pupil options.
   B. Pretend one corner of the room is the library center. Have some children select a book according to the procedures that have been

set up. All other members of the class should read in a book they have already selected.

C. The names of the students who conferenced yesterday should be on the chalkboard along with those for today. They will act as word helpers, hosts, and distributors of supplies and equipment.

D. Find a private area to conference and place a waiting chair nearby.

E. As the children come to the first conference scheduled, discuss with them briefly the types of things you will do with them during the conference.

F. After a child has had a conference, he may go to a hypothetical skills group based upon diagnosis in the conference.

G. After the skills class, the pupils may exercise an option of either going to a center of interest or making a book-sharing project. To make this part of the role-playing more meaningful, they could write out all of the things they would like to do at a writing center, science center, etc., or of the things that they would like to make for book-sharing.

H. Some of the children will enter in fully, while others will not. Note all of the things that went wrong during the session and discuss. They will probably center around the following concerns:

    1) I couldn't get a book because there were too many at the table.

    2) I didn't know what book to choose.

    3) John bothered me while I was reading.

    4) I didn't know a word and no one helped me.

    5) I didn't remember when I had a conference.

    6) I didn't know what to say to the teacher in the conference.

    7) I couldn't think of anything to write about at the center.

    8) What is a book-sharing project?

6. Some important considerations when organizing a classroom for personalized reading instruction are as follows:

A. Organize the room so heavy traffic is away from quiet areas like the library center.

B. Put the art center near a source of water.

C. Set up chairs for the conference in such a manner to give enough privacy to get the intimacy needed, yet within eyesight of the class.

D. Tables and chairs with book bins are usually more flexible than desks.

E. Islands of retreat should be provided for those who need them.

     F. Have easy access to supplies and equipment.

     G. Loud centers, such as woodworking, drama, and manipulative materials, should be set up in the hall or in another room.

7. Use the following for sharing in Uninterrupted Sustained Silent Reading:

     A. How many words were you reading per minute today? Was it better than yesterday? Did you lose anything in comprehension?

     B. Make a list of all the hard words.

     C. Find words in the book that represent a skill you are learning. (homonyms, synonyms, ch, sh, th, etc.)

     D. Summarize the book in one sentence or one paragraph.

     E. Keep a journal of interesting ideas.

     F. Describe a character in the book.

     G. Make a list of descriptive language.

     H. Ask a child to question you about your book.

     I. Share an interesting part orally to another class.

     J. Question the teacher about his/her book.

FOOTNOTES

[1]Norma Randolph, William Howe, and Elizabeth Achterman, *Self Enhancing Education: A Training Manual* (Santa Clara, California: Self Enhancing Education, Inc., 1971), p. 18.

[2]Jeannette Veatch, *Reading in the Elementary School* (New York, New York: The Ronald Press Co., 1966), p. 83.

[3]Lyman Hunt, "USSR: A Comment About the Most Basic Reading Skills" (Burlington, Vermont: University of Vermont Reading Center), p. 3.

[4]Hunt, "USSR," p. 2.

[5]Robert McCracken, *The Teaching of Reading* (Klamath Falls, Oregon: Klamath Printing Co., 1970), pp. 74-76.

[6]Hunt, "USSR," p. 3.

[7]Randolph, Howe, and Achterman, *Self Enhancing Education: A Training Manual*, p. 54.

[8]Randolph, Howe, and Achterman, *Self Enhancing Education: A Training Manual*, p. 55.

chapter three

Seeking, Self-Selecting, and Pacing in Personalized Reading Instruction

Common to most reading methodology is that the teacher selects for the child. To say that children can do better is to threaten a lot of well-meaning teachers of reading.

Research in the field of child development supports the contention that children in many areas of their lives will seek that which they need. In the teaching of reading this indicates that children can be trusted to seek those reading materials that are best for them. In fact, they will not only seek that which is best for them, but they will reject those materials which do not stimulate their best efforts.

Not long ago a large company selected professional readers to read every children's book they could find. After reading them they were to evaluate them and select the best 200. After this rather lengthy process, they placed the 200 books on library tables with books the children and teacher had selected together. Unknown to the children they marked the books that had been judged best by the "professionals." Much to their amazement, the children selected the books judged best by professionals only 33 percent of the time.

This is important to remember when selecting books for a classroom library center. If selection is done alone, it will be right about one-third of the time. If children are included in the selection process, a supply of books that will be of high interest to all will be more highly insured.

If the teacher checks out books from bookmobiles, city libraries, or college libraries, she should be sure to take the children along. Taking three or four children on a trip to the library, followed by a conversation break, has the added feature of building cohesion—something that is becoming more difficult every year for many of our classroom teachers.

Generalizations About Children's Interests

It is a well-known fact, for example, that bright and gifted elementary school children enjoy biographies. This is obviously explained by the fact that they like to identify themselves with successful people. Children of less innate ability, and often less actual reading ability, until a later age tend to prefer adventure stories. Poor readers usually prefer fast moving, action-filled stories. They usually like a single main character, without the use of too many descriptive adjectives, and they want a fast build-up to the conclusion. In addition to these rather distinctive characteristics and reading preferences of children of various mental levels, the various economic levels from which children come must also be considered. Children from lower economic levels understandably are often impatient with the well-dressed, over-indulged child found in many basal readers. Also, the child from a higher economic level often finds the stories, supposedly about this type of child, quite unlike reality.

Since it is not possible for any book to incorporate in the stories all the different types of children who will be reading the material, and meet all the particular reading needs found in any one classroom, the personalized method of reading allows the child to select those materials which do meet his needs and interests.

Collecting Reading Materials

Since the very basis of the personalized reading program is self-selection of materials which the pupil wants to and can read, a large supply of books covering many areas of interest and many different reading levels is absolutely essential. The teacher cannot hope to accumulate the many books necessary shortly before the program is to begin, for last-minute substitutions will mean books of less interest and, therefore, a less effective program.

The teacher beginning the personalized reading program may ask how many books should be available. In some ways this is a trap, as some critics of personalized reading take whatever numbers a given authority recommends, and generalize, "If you don't have ____ books per child, don't try it." And this is generally followed by other generalizations such as: "Don't do it if you don't have a lot of money, such and such a pupil-teacher ratio, a fully qualified librarian, a central library, etc."* If the self-selection approach for children is

---

*See Jerry L. Abbott, "Fifteen Reasons Why Personalized Reading Does Not Work," *Elementary English,* January 1972.

decided upon, the number of books necessary should not stand in the way. Even the poorest readers will read a book per week, so a lot of reading materials will be needed. The teacher should begin with what she has, and like a detective on a case, track down every possible clue that might lead her to books.

It seems that three books per child is a "rule of thumb" which is predominating the thinking of those who are operating successful personalized programs. This would mean a minimum of something over 100 books within the classroom at all times, and some of these 100 books will need to be rotated so that at the end of the year there will have been many more than just 100 titles in the room.

These 100 or more books will need to be in a wide variety of areas. One program described by Crossley and Kniley[1] tells of marking by color the field which each book specifically covered. Red meant that the book was general literature, while blue meant it was a basic book. Green meant it was science, and black meant social studies.

Jeannette Veatch reports that one primary teacher had a novel way of displaying books and at the same time taught alphabetizing by disregarding the content of the books, having each child look at the first letter of the title of the book he was using. Then around the window sills were placed enough wooden blocks as props for the books. The letters of the alphabet were thumbtacked onto them so that the books that began with "A" were placed just after the block that said "A." The books that began with "B" after "B," and so on.[2]

The number of copies of each book will perhaps vary. Apparently three copies of some titles are recommended at the primary levels. Teachers working in personalized programs in the upper elementary levels seem to suggest five or six copies of some books.

It is thought necessary by some teachers to mark the grade level on each book on the outside cover so that students can be guided to their approximate level. This seems to destroy some of the advantages of the self-selection process, however, for this is once again labeling reading levels as much as placing children in the slow, average, or fast group does. It must be recognized that many of the books will actually be very hard to classify as to the exact level because the vocabulary is not strictly controlled and because of what interest level does to reading level.

The range of difficulty will necessarily be great. At the higher levels, the range will have to increase. The teacher will have to judge the range depending upon her group, but it might be expected that primary one would include materials from the pre-primer level up to the intermediate four level. Early in the year, the majority of materials should be as low a level as possible, but as the children develop reading ability the teacher will need to collect more books from the primary one and two levels. The primary two program will have to go up to the intermediate five or six level and by sixth the range will probably be from primary one level all the way up through adult level books, with emphasis on the books at about intermediate six level.

How can a school possibly afford to buy all of the books that will be necessary in such a program? The answer is that in the first place there is no need to buy all of the books that will be needed, although there is certainly an advantage in having as many books as possible that actually stay in a particular classroom. Some books may be borrowed from children or checked out of the library.

The expense involved must be thought of in terms of the amount of money used to buy a single text for each child in the traditional program, plus the partial supplementary books which would probably number at least two or three per child. This money cannot be shifted over to purchasing library-type books immediately, but certainly over a period of time, it can be without any additional expense to the school system.

At first thought the teacher might feel that accumulating such a variety of books would be an almost impossible task. Sperber, in discussing a personalized reading program in primary three, makes this sound much easier when he mentions from where his books came. Each of his students joined the public library and was encouraged to bring books from there. Books were checked out from the traveling state education department library. Children brought books from their home libraries on loan for one year. An extra supply of the school library books was checked out. In addition to those checked out of the weekly trip of the entire class to the school library, the school collection of textbooks, supplementary readers, and basal readers, books from the college library and second-hand books purchased from the Salvation Army[3] provided additional sources.

Other sources where reading materials can be found are the following:

1. Newspaper publishers
2. Old magazines (Magazines such as *National Geographic* are particularly useful as many people collect them for long periods of time and then give them away.)
3. Book clubs
4. Parent groups who are interested in children's reading. (Right to Read, Reading is Fundamental, etc.)
5. Paperback collections that are no longer used because the children who once read them have grown up and left home
6. Sample copies of books from textbook companies
7. Book fairs
8. Second-hand stores
9. Purchase books from children

Getting books for the center and keeping a steady flow of reading materials is always a frightening experience for a classroom teacher. It is true that there are many fine sources from which the teacher can get books. Time, of course, is a problem. One way the teacher can insure a steady flow of reading material, yet not have to constantly be seeking books outside the school, is to gather a large paperback collection. These books should not be cataloged in any way. Rather, they can simply be placed in boxes, about 100 in each box, and divided only into primary paperbacks and intermediate paperbacks. Collecting can continue until the teachers have 2,000 or 3,000 books.

When the library center needs books, and the teacher does not have time to seek them outside the school, she can simply take a box of books, dump them on the library table, and feel good about the variety of selection.

In order for the personalized reading program to be successful, books which will interest children must be made available. For this reason classroom teachers must know a great deal about children's literature. Children's literature has long been one of the most popular courses offered in the teacher training program. Those teachers who have not had such a course should either take it from a nearby university, or can actually take the course by correspondence from almost any state university. If the teacher does not possess a wide knowledge of children's literature herself, there is little likelihood that she will inspire her students to love reading and books.

The Teacher's Role in Self-Selection

Determining the reading level of the children so that books may be available which they can read is one of the tasks of the teacher. This is not so difficult, or indeed even so important, as it is in the usual basal reader programs, however. In the process of self-selection of their own reading materials most pupils tend to select those books which they can read without too much difficulty. Generally, it is a good practice to prepare the pupils for the degree of ability expected in reading by indicating that for them to be able to read and comprehend they should encounter no more than three or four new words per page. This is sometimes explained in terms of errors and the same number, three or four per page, is considered maximum number.

Jeannette Veatch says it in another way which might work well with some children. She calls it the "Rule of Thumb." "Look over all the books. Pick out one that interests you. Rifle the pages and stop on one page in the middle of the book. Start to read it to yourself. If you come to a word that you don't know, put your thumb on the table. If you come to another word you don't know, put down your first finger. Another unknown word, another finger, and so on. If you use up all of your fingers, that book is too hard for you. Put it down and find another. If you find a book that has no unknown words, it is probably too easy for you. Save it for free time, and choose another book to bring to me for your conference.''[4]

Learning to choose the right book will necessarily take some time. It is nevertheless a skill which all children need to develop early. If it is learned well, then the periods which the children spend in the library will not be wasted. Learning to intelligently choose books to be read is a major feature of the personalized program. Although it cannot be measured in terms of any standardized tests, it is nevertheless a valuable and often overlooked skill. The child must be allowed to move freely to and from the spot where the books are collected so that he may exchange the book he has finished for another book at anytime.

When the personalized program is first beginning, the teacher should encourage each child to select the type of book which he wants to read and which he feels that he can read. She should then make use of all the information which she has about the child, and his reading ability, to determine if his selection of a book is in line with his ability to read and his interest. If it is not, the teacher should discuss with the child individually why this book was selected. It may be that the child can justify his selection. If he cannot, or if it appears as though he has merely picked a book because of an attractive cover or because someone else thrust it upon him, then the teacher should individually help him choose the right book.

Initially it may be necessary for the teacher to provide some guidance in assisting students in making the right selection, but once the pupil becomes accustomed to the procedure, little, if any, such help is necessary. If a pupil chooses books that are too hard or too easy, the teacher suggests that he choose other books which will be better for him. It is not absolutely necessary that he always read material at any exact level. When the other pupils have read books which they particularly liked, it is to be expected and desired that he will want to read them, even though they may be below his reading level. On the other hand, books along the line of a pupil's special interest will probably not be too difficult for him even if they are somewhat above his usual reading level.

Children are encouraged to read those books that they are able to read and that they want to read. This is absolutely essential in the personalized program if it is to have any advantage over the basal approach. Some suggestions from either the teacher or other children may be helpful, but are not absolutely necessary if the child feels free enough to try out as many books as he wants until he finds one that he can read and in which he is particularly interested.

Occasionally a child will read nothing but one kind of book or books by one author. As has been mentioned earlier, this is not to be discouraged. However, when one kind of book or one author so consumes a child as to give him tunnel vision, it is time to do some problem solving.

Some children have been observed reading nothing but *Hardy Boys* or *Nancy Drew* books. Others will read only books about horses, dinosaurs, fantasy, sports, or science fiction. One boy of the author's acquaintance read seventeen books by H. G. Wells. Upon looking at his cards it was found that, out of seventy-five, nearly all of them were about science. This is great. He was a vociferous reader, yet his topic was so narrow it began to affect his relationship with other children. No doubt, if this were to continue, he could have peer problems as he grew older. A boy like this needs to be worked with just as the child who doesn't read. And there is no better place to do this than in the individual conference.

Some teachers who are concerned about one-subject reading have made charts. bulletin boards, or reading wheels as a way to focus upon wide reading. One way to do this is to divide a large circle into as many divisions as there are reading categories and to place these categories (sports, mystery, science fiction, biography, etc.) on the wheel. Six or seven copies of each child's name can then be made. When he reads a book from a certain category, he pins his name in that section. A look at this chart periodically will instantly give him an idea of how widely he is reading.

Children's Choices

Sometimes it is worthwhile to ask each child to write down the name of the book he is currently reading. A survey of these book titles will give the classroom teacher a good idea of what kind of things children are reading, the variety they seek, the instructional level they are at, possibilities for instruction in other areas of the curriculum, and the tremendous diversity you have in your classroom. Following is a list of books found in the hands of a group of intermediate six children about midway through the school year:

Title	Author
Model Rockets for Beginners	Horace Gilmore
Johnny Unitas Story	Lee Greene
Daredevils of the Speedway	Ross Olney
Rickenbacker	Eddie Rickenbacker
Little Women	Louisa May Alcott
Baseball's Greatest Players	Tom Meany
Skeleton Cave	Cora Cheney
Mystery of the Old Dutch Chest	Gloria Savoldi
Who Goes Next: True Stories of Strange Escapes	Robert Alter
Stories of Champions	Sam Epstein
Laughing Matter	Helen Smith
Lad of Sunnybank	Albert Payson Terhune
Instant Replay–The Greenbay Diary of Jerry Kramer	Jerry Kramer

Dinny Gordon	Anne Emery
Action in Submarine	Arthur Widder
How to Care for Your Dog	Jean Bethell
Skiing	Leonard Shortall
Secret Agent Four	Donald Sobal
Red Skeleton's Favorite Ghost	
Stories	Red Skeleton
Beetle Bailey	Mort Walker
Hit Parade of Sport Stories	Dick Friendlich
Rocket: How It Works	David Corey
Baseball Stories	Frank Owen
Doctor Dolittle	Hugh Lofting
All of a Kind Family	Sydney Taylor
Wild Wheels	Don McKay

Summary

Personalized Reading Instruction is a philosophy of teaching reading that relies heavily upon Willard C. Olson's principles of seeking, self-selecting, and pacing.

In this chapter we have stated several important factors related to children's interests, given teachers many ideas for seeking new sources of books, and discussed some important factors relative to teacher behavior in personalized reading.

Seeking, Self-Selection, and Pacing IDEA Bank

1. Each week select a "Book of the Week." This is the book judged best by the children. You can make this even more interesting by having a "Book of the Month," and "Book of the Year." Write to the author and congratulate him when his book has been chosen.

2. Think of as many catchy sentences as you can to advertise the library center. (Take a Book from the Reading Nook) (Try It, You'll Like It) (It's the Real Thing)

3. Talk to the class about book reviews: where they come from, how to find them, how to use them.

4. Talk with the class about ways to use a book jacket.

5. Study the life of an author.

6. Talk about the purposes of: The Table of Contents, Illustration, The Appendix, The Introduction, and the Index.

7. Form a parents' committee on books. You might call it the "Book

Scrounging Committee.'' Select one interested parent as the chairman. He in turn selects three other members. When your supply of books gets low, call the chairman who will in turn put the committee to work. You might be surprised how many books they can find.

8. Make a list of factors that determine why children select certain books. It might help you with children who are reluctant about self-selection. Some will be: (1) illustrations and pictures; (2) content; (3) size of the book and/or print; (4) recommendations of other students; (5) the attractiveness of, or what is written on the book jacket; (6) the ease of reading; (7) interesting things about the author; (8) fulfillment of a research need.

9. Helping children with unknown words can take a lot of valuable time and be very disrupting to the conference. Make the following chart as a way to economize time and assure good conferences without interruptions:

A GOOD COMBINATION UNLOCKS NEW WORDS

1. Use picture clues.

2. Use context clues.

3. Search for a root word.

4. Divide the word into syllables.

5. Look it up in the glossary or dictionary.

6. If the lock doesn't open, ask someone.

7. Sometimes you should: "skip it; any author worth his salt will make the point again.''

---

10. Increase the focus on silent reading by involving the entire school in Uninterrupted Sustained Silent Reading. On a given day, and at a given time, Uninterrupted Sustained Silent Reading is announced over the intercom. Everyone drops what they are doing and reads the book of their choice.

11. Invite the librarians from the bookmobile in once per month to give you reviews of the latest books for children.

12. Another way to assure the correct fit between the child's reading level and his chosen book is to retype a story that is of high interest to the child. Leave every fifth word blank. Have the child read the

selection, supplying the printed word. Older children can write the words in, younger children can read the passage to you. Their score is determined by counting as correct responses the number of words actually used by the author. A score of 40 percent or better indicates the child can handle the book. Below that indicates the book may be too difficult for the child.

FOOTNOTES

[1]Ruth Crossley and Mildred Kniley, "An Individualized Reading Program," *Elementary English*, Vol. 41, January 1959, pp. 16-20.

[2]Jeannette Veatch, *Reading in the Elementary School* (New York, New York: The Ronald Press, Co., 1966), p. 84.

[3]Robert Sperber, "An Individualized Reading Program in a Third Grade," *Individualized Reading Practices*, Alice Meil, ed., No. 14, Practical Suggestions for Teaching (New York: Bureau of Publications, Teachers College, Columbia University), p. 47.

[4]Veatch, *Reading in the Elementary School*, p. 41.

chapter four

Developing the Conference as an Essential Aid to Reading Instruction

No phase of the personalized program is so important as the individual conference: everything that comes before it leads to it, and everything that comes after it is the result of it. It is at this time that the teacher either successfully reaches the child and succeeds in teaching him to read, or fails to reach him and therefore fails to aid him in becoming a better reader. And the individual conference, although unique to personalized or individualized reading, can be used in any reading program. In fact, teachers could greatly improve reading instruction if they were to utilize the individual conference in whatever reading program they are using.

The individual conference is a private one-to-one relationship between the pupil and the teacher through which the teacher attempts to assess the child's reading skills in order to direct reading growth and to assure each child that reading will be both pleasurable and exciting for as long as he lives. Jeannette Veatch summarizes the conference by saying: "No part of the curriculum, no classroom activity, can begin to compare with the warmth of human relationship in a one-to-one conference. When the climate of learning has an element of personal warmth, the learning is faster, easier, and more permanent."[1]

Like any other technique, the conference has been both misunderstood and misused. A common misunderstanding relates to the amount of teacher time spent in a one-to-one relationship with the children. Failing to internalize the complete program, some teachers see much needless repetition as the result of meeting children individually. Another problem is that some teachers have

59

failed to see the individual conference as an important and complex skill that must constantly be refined and improved. They don't read much themselves and rely upon canned, convergent questions; they do most of the talking; overuse oral reading, and most importantly refuse to learn the reading skills well enough so they can pinpoint children's strengths and weaknesses.

There is no technique any better than those who are using it. The purpose of this chapter is to identify the important components of the conference, and help teachers sharpen their skills to utilize it better.

Getting the Conference Underway

In the beginning stages of the program most teachers structure their conferences quite carefully. Once they have built confidence and the children know what they are to do, they move away from this structure and build more voluntary components into the program.

The teacher usually places herself off to one part of the room away from other children with a seat for the child beside her. She may either be at a desk or a table. With children in the primary levels the teacher will most likely want to sit with the children either at a table or in a chair their size so that the relationship will not be one across a formal desk. Even with upper elementary children, this same procedure is often advisable. In no instance would it be wise to seat the child across the desk if this meant that the child was so far removed from the teacher that he had to speak loudly. Such loud speaking would not only interrupt other children but also tend to embarrass the child if he made a mistake.

The conference should be as nearly as possible a very individual thing, without anyone overhearing. It is likely that the children could hear if they wanted to, but the goal would be to have them so busily engaged in their own activities that they would not care to listen.

Each day the teacher puts on the chalkboard the names of those students with whom she wishes to conference. The previous day's names stay on the board. These students become word helpers, hosts and hostesses, and distributors of equipment and supplies. The purpose of this is to free the teacher from all needless interruptions and give the program structure.

In order that there will be minimum amount of time wasted between conferences, a seat somewhere nearby, but still at a great enough distance so that the conference is not interfered with, is occupied by the child who will see the teacher next. This seat, sometimes referred to as the "next at bat" or "on deck" chair, is filled by the child assigned for the next conference.

The length of time which a child spends with his teacher varies from five to 15 minutes, depending upon the teacher's proficiency at conferencing and the areas to be covered. In the beginning stages of conferencing it is not uncommon to take up to 15 minutes for a conference. Once proficiency has been gained, each conference will take about five minutes.

If the reading period is from 60 to 90 minutes, about one-half of it should be devoted to conferences. This means meeting about one-third of the class per day which will give them contact with the teacher once every three or four days. Conferencing with each child one time per week is considered a minimum. Anything less will disappoint and disinterest the children.

Teachers continue to report that time is their greatest enemy. They simply do not find the time to conference as much as the children desire. This problem can be overcome by looking to others for help. Student teachers, teacher aides, parent aides, and other students have all been used with great success. Of course, some time needs to be spent training these people both in technique and the underlying philosophy of personalized reading instruction.

Scheduled Versus Unscheduled Conferences

There is some disagreement as to whether conferences should be scheduled or voluntary. Some people recommend allowing students to come voluntarily at the time they have either need for help from the teacher or something which they particularly want to share with the teacher. In such a situation, if certain children do not voluntarily come to see the teacher once every three or four days, the teacher asks them to come for a conference.

When conferences are voluntary, there is the advantage of a child conferencing to meet a felt need. Avid readers might have several conferences the same day or the same week. However, the other side of that is the shy, retiring child who is not so assertive, and therefore does not come as often as he should. The keeping of careful records by a perceptive teacher can relieve this problem. However, more important than the child who comes for conferences too often, or not often enough, is what voluntary conferences do to the teacher's time. If voluntary conferences are used, the teacher must be very careful and precise in both diagnosis and record-keeping to insure systematic skill instruction.

There are advantages of both methods of scheduling conferences. The teacher may capitalize upon the advantages by employing both kinds of conferences by using the scheduled kind to insure the continuous growth of skills and the voluntary conferences when many children have a great need to share what they are reading. On days when the latter situation occurs, the teacher may dispense with the regular conferences and say, "Today I would like to conference with anyone who would like to share something with me. Sign up on the board." A position between the two extremes would be to schedule conferences and leave a couple of blanks for those who feel as though they must see the teacher.

Advantages of Individual Conferences

As indicated earlier, conferences are no better than those using them. Given an enthusiastic teacher who is constantly concerned about her conferencing skills, the following positive things should result:

1. *Individual Differences:*

   Obviously, nothing has the power to treat individual differences as does a situation where the child and the teacher meet on a one-to-one basis. There is simply no limitation on how far and how fast a child can go in his reading.

2. *Guidance Function:*

   Teachers continue to report that they never knew their children so well as when they begin to meet them individually. No teacher is asked to be a therapist. Rather, the climate in which the conference takes place, together with the material that is discussed, has terrific potential both to put the child in a relaxed mood and to improve his self-image. Because children oftentimes select reading material which is closely related to their lives, a therapeutic effect is achieved as the child solves his own problems through those of a character in a book.

3. *Discipline:*

   Almost every research study that has been undertaken in the area of personalized reading indicates that children are easier to handle when they conference regularly with their teacher. The intimate relationship, together with the child working at his individual interest and achievement level, is no doubt the reason.

4. *Interest:*

   Any survey of children's interests reveals a scope so broad as to make it impossible to meet their needs in any other way but self-selection and individual conferences. There is simply no reason why each child cannot be pursuing his own interests in this program.

5. *Love for Reading:*

   One of the major reading problems today is the children who can read, but don't. Basal readers, together with teachers who have not understood their goals, have no doubt contributed to this deficiency. When a child comes to the conference with a self-selected book, there is ample opportunity to improve both his reading skills and his desire to read.

6. *Skills:*

   A strength of the conference is that each child's skill needs can be pinpointed without regard to the rest of the class. There simply isn't any reason why a child should be in a group learning skills that he already knows, or be frustrated by trying to learn skills that are too difficult for him.

7. *Professional Growth of Staff:*

Teachers involved in personalized reading report a professional stimulation rarely found in any reading program. Their knowledge of children's literature increases phenomenally; they learn the reading skills in a more thorough way; and they feel good about their new role as diagnostician.

8. *Competition:*

When a child conferences with his teacher about his progress, he learns about his successes and failures in such a way that they are measured against himself and not his peers.

9. *Reading in the Content Areas:*

A survey of children's choices reveals interest so broad as to include most of the content areas. There is no reason why a teacher cannot constantly relate what a child is reading to every other area of the curriculum.

10. *Labeling:*

One of the most severe criticisms of the basal approach to reading has been inflexible groupings in which children are placed in a group for the entire year. Teachers try to reduce the "sting" of the label by using such words as "bluebirds," "redbirds," and "astronauts." Of course, they fool no one. The children know which group is "slow," "middle," and "fast" and frequently refer to it by these labels in spite of the teacher's efforts to call it something else. The conference labels no one. Neither does what follows. As the child leaves the conference, he is either directed to self-instructional materials, or is placed in a temporary group, the reason for which he understands. There is no reason to label any child.

Problems Posed by the Individual Conference

Like anything else, all is not positive. There are problems associated with the conference. However, with constant attention and refinement of the process, they can be overcome.

1. *Conferencing with a Book You Haven't Read:*

One of the most common problems associated with the conference, especially in the beginning, is that of conferencing about a book which hasn't been read. In a situation like this some teachers say, "Tell me about your book," or "What part of the book would you like to tell someone about who hadn't read the book?" Because this is a rather low level of questioning, the teacher should learn about the contents of the book as rapidly as possible. Of course, the longer teachers are involved in this type of program, the more they will learn about children's books. After seven years in personalized reading, one teacher reports she knows the contents of about 70 percent of the books children bring to the conference. Some other methods of learning about the contents of books include the following:

1) reading books that one would read to children.

2) taking children's literature courses at a college or university.

3) asking the librarian to write reviews of books she has read.

4) beginning a hobby of collecting and reading children's books.

5) forming a club of interested parents or senior citizens to read and review children's books.

6) reading book summaries made by children.

7) listening to summaries that children have put on tape.

8) listening to tape recordings and records that now accompany many books.

9) learning as much as possible about authors.

10) reading reviews by professional reviewers.

11) reading summaries found on book jackets.

2. *The Child Who Misunderstands the Shift from Basal Readers to Self-Selected Books:*

Again, in the beginning stages of the program, it is not uncommon for some children to have problems internalizing the idea that the self-selected book is, in fact, their reading book. They evidence this by bringing books to the conference that are at frustration level, that are consistently at recreational level, or that haven't been read. These are not major problems, and can be overcome by a patient and understanding teacher. For the very young child, or shy child, it might take some time to explain that this is their reading book and they must prepare for the conference just like they did for the basal reading classes. If a child brings to the conference a book which he just started and does not yet know anything about it, he can simply be reminded that he should bring to conference the last book he read.

3. *Children Who Forget to Come for Conference:*

A problem created by children who forget to come for conference can be overcome by scheduling conferences. However, if the teacher feels strongly about voluntary conferences she will need to find some technique for the forgetful child that will remind him to conference every three or four days. If five or six children are making voluntary conferences difficult, the teacher should group them and work on the problem, or schedule their conferences.

4. *Teachers Who are Afraid of the Skills Program:*

One of the most common problems associated with the conference is a fear on the part of teachers that they are not presenting a systematic program of skill development. The basal reader manuals give them a great sense of security and assurance that skills are being taught. Some authorities in reading say it is all but impossible to break through this defense mechanism. These teachers do not feel as though they have the expertise to diagnose adequately a child's skill needs and to offer suitable alternatives. Some teachers have met this problem and have overcome it by making a slow transition from the basal reader skills program to their own. They use all facets of the personalized program except the part which calls for them to diagnose the skill needs of children. Instead, they continue to follow the skills program of the basal readers. They present skills to groups and regroup those children who did not achieve mastery. Then, after they feel more secure with the program, they begin to move away from the basal program and, within a short time, rely completely upon their own ingenuity and use the basal materials only when they meet a particular need. This method of skill instruction would no doubt be held in suspect by some reading authorities. However, if this is what it takes to make the transition from basal reading to personalized reading, the teacher should do it.

5. *Record-Keeping:*

One of the common problems of the individual conference is that of record-keeping. The keeping of good records is at the very heart of good diagnosis because they give the teacher an ongoing record of strengths and weaknesses as well as interests. Therefore, it is imperative that teachers develop a system that is simple and quick, yet thorough enough to provide all the information that is needed and diagnostic enough to be helpful.

6. *Time:*

Many teachers have, in fact, rejected personalized reading because of the time involved in individual conferences. When one analyzes the time each child receives in basal reading, it works out to be about the same. As in personalized reading it must be remembered that besides one or two five minute conferences per week, each child will have ample opportunity to interact with his teacher in skill and interest groups, in group conferences, and whole class groups. The only way to look at time is not that "there is never enough time," but "all I have is time."

For Teachers New at Conferencing

Most teachers have a lot of experience working with groups, but very little in a one-to-one situation. So, like any other new skill, the conference must be practiced and refined until it becomes internalized.

What can teachers do to become more proficient at conferencing? First, it is wise to recall some of the principles of building the entwining relationship with others. Children perceive the world much differently than do adults. By using the children as a unique resource, and continually asking, "What about the conference gave you a good feeling, and what about the conference gave you concerns?", teachers can be assured of congruence with respect to perception.

Sending and Receiving Messages

The importance of being a good listener cannot be overemphasized. The teacher should try to assess her listening skills. She should time herself in a conference. If the teacher finds she is spending more than half of the conference time talking, she has probably not yet developed sufficient listening skills.

How the teacher listens is also important. She must try to hook into children's feelings and really begin to know how it is with them and listen to them at the feeling level. When conferencing with a child, the teacher must listen carefully to what he is saying. She may hook into the feelings by using the following process:

1) deciding whether what he is saying is pain or pleasure.

2) finding a word that best describes that pain or pleasure.

3) using that word in a sentence or a question in such a way as to require a response from the child.[2]

The process could go something like this:

Child: "The little girl opened the cabin door and the doorway was filled by a huge black bear!"

Teacher: "It must be *frightening* to stare into the eyes of a bear?"

Child: "That happened to my dad and me one time when we were taking things to the dump."

This technique, known as reflective listening, is a very good tool to use to know how it is with another person. It requires the teacher to reserve judgment until she allows the other person to state his feeling condition. Then the teacher can send her feeling condition, and possibly ask for solutions if they are required.

How messages are sent is as important as good listening. Some authorities in the area of communications are now saying that up to 57 percent of all communication is non-verbal. If that is correct, teachers need to spend time assessing how they speak to children non-verbally. Voice intonation, facial expressions, and gestures all speak very loudly to the child. Non-verbal messages to the child should be sent congruently. This means that the non-verbal part of the message should say the same thing as the verbal part. Failure to do this places the child in a double bind, and getting a response from him will be difficult.

There is also need to be forthright with children. In order to confront others we must feel good about ourselves. When confronting in an entwining way, bonds of trust are built with the other person.

Another important communications skill for the teacher who wishes to be successful in working with children in the conference is that of dealing with the universal message. The universal message is a sweeping generalization, usually very judgmental and evaluative, about which the receiver is helpless to solve until he gets the sender to "own" the message. For instance, if a child says, "Conferences are boring," the wise teacher will change that message into one of ownership by either asking the child to "own the feeling," ("I feel conferences are boring.") or better still, reflecting it with: "Something about the way I conduct conferences really upsets you?" To that the child might reply, "Yeh, we spend too much time with the skills and I don't get enough time to tell you about the story."

Now the problem has the potential to be solved. Universal messages tend to place the sender and the receiver in a power struggle with a winner and a loser. On the other hand, if the teacher uses the skills previously described, there is some assurance that the child will begin to reveal his feeling condition more often. When this happens a bond will develop between the teacher and the child and hopefully, fewer instances of inappropriate communication.*

Kinds of Conferences

One-to-One Conferences

This is the type of conference that has been described in detail and lies at the heart of personalized reading. It is the use of this technique that will determine success in personalized reading instruction. The teacher should plan to spend about one-half of the reading period meeting children in one-to-one conferences.

Group Conferences with the Same Book

It is true that meeting children in a one-to-one setting has a powerful effect upon them. However, there is no reason why group conferences cannot be

---

*Reflective listening, congruence, forthrightness, and the universal message are all part of Self Enhancing Education. They can be studied in depth through training materials that have been developed. Contact Self Enhancing Education, Inc., 1957 Pruneridge Avenue, Santa Clara, California.

utilized. There are currently many opportunities for several children to be reading the same book. Paperback book clubs, books with accompanying tapes and records, and inexpensive hardback books all make it possible to have several copies of the same book. Add to this the listening centers found in most classrooms today, and it is not only possible, but quite probable, that several children will be reading the same book at the same time.

The teacher may gather several copies of the same book until five or six copies of several titles have been collected. She should try to find titles that are of high interest to the children. On a given morning, she may talk briefly about each of the titles, asking the children to select the book which seems to interest them most. Some will select a book because they are genuinely interested in the topic, while others will base their selection upon choices made by peers. This is not important; what is important is that each child has a book and is reading it. When all members of a group are reading the same book, questioning can be done in the same manner as in the individual conference. An advantage of this type of conference is that children have an opportunity to challenge each other's ideas, and the consolidation of selections allows conferences long enough to become thoroughly engrossed in the contents of the book. The disadvantage, of course, is that the limited number of books violates the principle of self-selection.

Group Conferences with Different Books

There will be times when the children indicate that they want more time with the teacher. On these days the teacher may ask them to sign up for a group conference and explain that even though each child will have a different book, it is still possible to have a worthwhile conference. A degree of homogeneity can be attained by asking the children to sign up according to topics such as mystery, biography, fiction, etc. This will, to some extent, reduce the scope of the questions.

Although many of the questions appropriate in other types of conferences can be used, some care should be taken. For instance, if a mechanical question such as prefixes, suffixes, root words, or syllables is asked, any child could easily make an appropriate response. If, on the other hand, a comprehension question is asked, some thought will be required to assure a question that has meaning to the entire group. Some questions that might be used for this type of conference are as follows:

1. Who wants to share the most exciting part of his book?
2. All of you have been grouped for this conference because you have biographies. Who can tell me what a biography is?
3. Did you find any words you didn't know? What are they? Let's make a list.

4. Who would like to tell about the most interesting character in his book?

5. What would you like to share about the author of your book?

6. How would you sum up your book in one sentence?

7. What about the book made you feel good? Gave you concerns?

8. Do you know of anyone in real life who resembles a character in your book? Tell us about him.

9. How do you think the characters in your book would cope with life today?

10. Does the book speak to us today? How?

11. Who would like to ask one of the other group members about his book?

12. Now that we have talked about all of your books, what did they seem to have in common? How were they different?

Whole Class Conferencing Each with a Different Book

Uninterrupted Sustained Silent Reading is an example of a time when it is very appropriate to conference with the entire class. See Chapter two for ideas to organize for Uninterrupted Sustained Silent Reading and appropriate questions to ask.

What Happens in the Conference?

Because conferencing is a very open-ended activity, there is no prescribed way for it to proceed. However, there are general guidelines that have been found to be helpful.

First, it is important that teachers do not feel as though they need to check everything. Because of the great amount of reading that is accomplished, the teacher should plan to conference on one out of each six to eight books the child reads. Trying to check everything a child reads is a hopeless task for the teacher and a denial of the fact that children should be responsible for their own learning.

One of the most debatable questions related to the individual conference is that of whether the conference is a time to diagnose or a time to instruct. A survey of teachers using this method of reading indicates they use the conference both for diagnosis and instruction. Phonics skills, unknown words, vocabulary development, etc. are usually worked with at the beginning of the conference, leaving the remainder of the time for comprehension and oral reading. These teachers further indicate that as they become more proficient in the use of the conference they can begin to determine what should be taught during the conference and what should be saved for group teaching. For instance, if a child is having trouble unlocking a word that would give added meaning to the story, it would be wise to teach it on the spot. If, on the other hand, the problem is that of not understanding vowel sounds, it should be noted and taught at some later date in a group with other children who have the same problem.

Children who have reading problems oftentimes have an accompanying problem of low self-image. This problem can be compounded by a continual emphasis upon weaknesses. Many times the best way to improve a reading problem is to first find the child's strengths, and work through them.

It is particularly important that this individual period not become just another oral reading session, different only from reading in a circle procedure in that no one is listening but the teacher and the material is not the usual textbook. This is not an oral reading period, although it is naturally assumed that more oral reading will be expected from the primary children than from the intermediate children.

Teachers often ask about the emphasis oral reading should have during the conference. Advice from experts ranges all the way from leaving it to other parts of the reading program, to never having a conference without making oral reading its high point. As the teacher becomes proficient in the use of the conference she will be in the best position to determine appropriate emphasis in oral reading. Certainly the teacher will want to use oral reading during many of her conferences. When used, it is important that the teacher know why she wants the child to read orally and accept nothing but the child's best efforts. Poor oral reading is worse than none.

Children are enthusiastic about reading orally to their teacher. The conference is a perfect setting for oral reading because there is no fear of mistakes. When used correctly—that is, oral reading preceded by silent reading and preparation for oral reading—the teacher can learn much about where the child is experiencing difficulties. It is also the perfect technique for sharing something that can be best comprehended when it is read orally.

As the teacher discusses the material with the child, gets to know him and his reading habits and interests better, she records pertinent information on the child's record. In addition to checking his comprehension and the level of difficulty of the material he is reading, she will probably also check his ability with particular words in the story that are difficult. (The students themselves may have prepared the list of difficult words from the story as they read it and brought this list to the conference.) All of this is recorded, as is the child's ability to use successfully the particular word attack skills felt to be necessary at the level at which he is reading. Such skills might include sounds of certain letters, seeing small words inside large words, etc.

But the teacher is also responsible for watching for the child with emotional difficulties. It is not meant to imply that in the personalized reading program the teacher is expected to be able to cure severe emotional problems, for she certainly cannot. But the teacher is in an advantageous position to come to know the student better individually, and to talk over with him any problems he may want to discuss with her. This added time with children individually should put the teacher in a better position to know when to refer particular children for any kind of special attention, whether it might be for special work in reading, speech correction work, mental testing to determine potentiality, or any other type of special referral.

The individual conference period may well be a remedial period for some children. The child who is far below the class level in reading may require very easy material in order to find success. In the personalized program, he is better able to find satisfaction in reading at his own level without the embarrassment of having to stumble along in material that is too difficult in front of his fellow classmates. But in order to help him, the teacher may have to work with him on basic skills of a very early level or even at a readiness level. The advantage of the individual conference is that the teacher will at least have some time, admittedly too limited but nevertheless more than in the usual program, to work with the remedial reading case alone and in small groups with other children at his level.

The conference must not become a testing period for which the child feels he must prepare. It is instead a relaxed discussion period during which time the child and the teacher share experiences together. Too formalized a procedure will result in the conference being less successful.

Developing the Art of Inquiry

Developing the art of inquiry is the most important part of the individual conference. Lists of questions, helpful as they are, can only serve as a source of ideas. What questions to ask, and when to ask them, will come with practice and is the key to developing the art of inquiry.

The success of a conference is many times determined by how it begins. When a child comes for a conference the teacher should say something, both verbally and non-verbally, to let him know that she is excited about the possibilities of the next few minutes. Sometimes it may be appropriate to begin by asking him a question about his book, and other times it might be appropriate to ask him about some other subject area, something that happened in the classroom, or his peers, or whatever seems to kick off feelings in the child. Statements like the following are all good ways to set the stage for a successful conference:

"You really like horse stories, don't you?"

"Wow, What a big book. Did you ever think you would finish it?"

"You must really like Beverly Cleary."

"I was really proud of the way you gave that report, Bill."

"I had a nice visit with your mom when she worked in our classroom this morning, Mary."

The idea is to say or do something that will relax the child in such a way as to make him want to share his reading. Again, as proficiency is attained in conferencing, these questions will come automatically.

What kinds of questions should be asked during the conference? The teacher should try to get as much divergence as possible. Open-endedness, divergence, mind stretching, and reading between the lines is the goal of good comprehension. The use of convergent comprehension questions is recommended when they will lead to divergence. The teacher should ask questions that relate to a child's backlog of experiences for it is easier to speak from experience. The teacher should also discourage the child's parroting back what the author said and should try to make the child confront the author with his own opinion.

It is always interesting to get the child's reaction to the book. One way of doing this is to find out if he sees things the way the author did and if he would have changed the story in any way. The teacher may discuss appealing, humorous, sad, or important parts of the book. It is at this time when it might be appropriate to ask the child to select the part he likes best and to read it orally.

Hopefully, teachers of personalized reading utilize language experience activities in their classrooms. Using the experiences of children not only lays a good foundation for individual authorship, but heightens interest in reading as well. From the very beginning, children should have been relating their experiences to their teacher, and the teacher should be using these experiences to improve their reading. With this kind of background, together with a heavy emphasis upon creative writing, the child should be very comfortable with the conference. No child should leave the elementary school without internalizing the fact that his vast storehouse of experiences gives him a perfect reason to continue reading and writing.

Most research related to the amount of time children are given to answer questions makes two things very clear: (1) teachers don't give children enough time to answer questions; and, (2) girls get more time to answer than boys. The teacher should not get excited about covering material. Even though five minute conferences sometimes seem short, children should be given ample time to answer questions.

Another problem is the tendency of teachers to be too judgmental and at inappropriate times. Some of the questions asked in a conference require the teacher to be judgmental, while others do not. For instance, if a child is asked to unlock a word which he doesn't know, and he says it incorrectly, it is legitimate to judge. (Sometimes he is half right and should be rewarded for that.) If, on the other hand, the child is asked what the author might have been thinking when he wrote a certain passage, it would be wrong to ask the child to perceive the event in the same way the teacher perceives it.

It is unlikely that children will get excited about the conference unless the teacher appreciates good literature. It is, of course, hoped that the child will gain this appreciation from the enjoyment he finds from reading material which he has selected himself. But the process of self-selection alone does not develop an appreciation for reading if the child does not feel this appreciation from the teacher herself. More than in any other type of program, the teacher's attitude toward reading will affect the attitude of the children in the classroom. If the teacher is one who is too busy to find time to read herself, then it is not likely that she will take full advantage of the individual conference and develop good attitudes toward reading. Only if the teacher herself truly appreciates literature, including adult literature as well as children's literature, can it be expected that the child will "catch" the joy of reading.

When questioning children about the contents of their books, there is a tendency on the part of the teacher to want closure. Many activities during the school day require the teacher to summarize and bring them to closure. This should not always be the case when questioning children about their reading. At times the child should make the closing comments about his book. To always require the last word is to dull the fine art of inquiry.

How conferences end is just as important as how they begin. In the closing minutes of the conference the teacher and the child should be thoroughly engrossed in the contents of the book. Because a strength of the conference is that it determines what comes next, they should have made decisions about some of the following:

1) Where are my skill needs? (Strengths as well as weaknesses)
2) Are these provided for through self-assignment, or must I meet in a group?
3) What kinds of choices should I make about future reading?
4) How should I share my reading with others?
5) What should I write in my records?

As the conference comes to a close, there should be a relaxed mood in which both the teacher and the child feel good about what has taken place. The teacher should have learned something about the child's strengths, weaknesses and interests; and the child should have been enlarged and given some help to know what comes next.

Questions for the Conference

There are currently many fine lists of questions that can be used in the conference. In the beginning stages of conferencing, the teacher should plan to seek out some of these lists and place them on cards. She should arrange the questions around such topics as word attack, comprehension, attitudes, etc. for easy access to questions that meet a certain need. Before too long the teacher will have more questions in her mind than she does on cards, and the cards can be discarded.

Dr. Lyman Hunt likes to separate questioning into three categories: (1) Appropriateness of the Book; (2) Appreciation of the Book; (3) Values Gained from the Book. In the area of appropriateness he tries to get at such things as: "Why did you choose the book?", "Was it hard, easy, or just right?" and "Would you choose the book again?" Appreciation deals with where, along a continuum from best liked to least liked, would you place the book: "Was the book good?", "What made it good?" or "Would you read the book again?" are examples. Values gained from the book are designed to go into depth about ideas found in the book: "Did something happen in the book that you would like to have happen to you?", "Give me the high points." or "What do you think the person who wrote the book was trying to say?" are questions that try to get at meaning.[3]

A survey of teachers using personalized reading instruction indicates wide use of the following questions:

Comprehension

1. What kind of a story was this? (fact, fiction, fable, myth, comedy, epic, etc.)
2. Who was the main character in the book? Tell me about him.
3. What specific things do you recall about: (1) the setting of the story, (2) the characters, (3) interesting language, (4) the ending, (5) illustrations.
4. Where did the story take place? How can you tell?
5. You seem to like books about heroes. Who do you think was the hero in this book? What makes you think so?
6. Can you find the main idea in this paragraph? This chapter?
7. Who was the author writing about in this book? Is the author writing about people who lived long ago or today? How can you tell?
8. Why do you think the author chose this title? What other titles could you think of?
9. What one thing did you learn that you didn't know before?

10. Did you agree with the author's conclusion? Why or why not?

11. If you could change part of the story, what would you change? Why?

12. Did any pictures help you understand the book? Which ones? How?

13. What does this sentence mean?

14. Can you show me how the author indicated sadness, happiness, action?

15. Can you find any figures of speech? What do they mean?

16. Was there anything in the book that was difficult to understand? What?

17. Can you find an example of exaggeration in this book?

Word Analysis

1. Could you find some words that you didn't know? What makes them difficult?

2. Did you find any words that had one meaning in one part of the story and another in a different part of the story?

3. How do you unlock words that you don't know?

4. How does this word begin? End?

5. What is a root word? Can you find some?

6. What is a prefix? A suffix? Can you find some?

7. Can you divide this word into syllables?

8. What is a compound word? Can you find one?

9. Can you think of a rhyming word for this word?

10. What two words does this contraction stand for?

11. What letters are silent in this word?

Attitudes and Values

1. You really seem to admire _____ in this book? Why is that?

2. Do you know anyone who reminds you of characters in this book? Who? Why?

3. Have you read other stories that ended this way? Why do you like stories that have this kind of ending?

4. Would you like to have a friend like one of the characters in the book? Which one? Why?

5. Why do you think the author likes to write about _____? (Horses sports, cars, etc.)

6. Why do you like this author?

7. Why did you select this book?

8. Would you recommend this book? Why?

9. Did anything happen in this book that you would like to have happen to you? What? Why?

10. How did you feel when you read . . . . . ?

11. Have you ever had a problem like the character in this book? Tell me about it.

12. What part of the book would you like to read to me? Why did you choose this part?

13. What about the story made you want to continue reading it?

14. Can you find something from the book that indicates how the characters spoke?

15. Can you find the funniest part and tell me about it?

16. If a classmate asked about this book, would you recommend it? Why? Why not?

How One Teacher Looks at Conferencing

The question often asked is: "Do conferences get boring after a while?" In other words, as the teacher moves from three group teaching in a basal reader to a method which calls for half of the reading time to be spent in conferences, is there not a danger of the conference becoming routine?

Teachers involved in personalized reading report that conferences do not get boring. The open-endedness of the questioning, together with the principle of self-selection, continually brings excitement and enthusiasm to each conference.

One teacher interviewed had been involved in personalized reading for seven years. During that time it is estimated that she has spent over 35,000 minutes in individual conferences. She reports that sameness and routine, the old enemies of the basal reader, are rarely a problem. The intimate relationship, found only in the conferences, creates a setting in which each is enlarged.

Conference Checklist

An attempt has been made to identify the important components of the conference and discuss them in detail. The following checklist will help determine readiness to begin the conference:

Conference Check List

YES	NO	SOMETIMES	Circle	1	2	3	4	5	6	7	8	9	10	Conference Number
			1.											Did you explain the "Plan for the day" so each child knows what to do?
			2.											Are the children settled into the "Plan for the day?"
			3.											Is the room organized correctly?
			4.											Do those who are to conference know how to prepare for the conference?
			5.											Do those who are to conference known when to come?
			6.											Have you decided the thrust of the conference for each child?
			7.											Are your records in order?
			8.											Have you gathered all of the materials that you will need? (record sheets, books, child's folder, etc.)
			9.											Do you have some hunches about the "next step" for those with whom you will conference?
			10.											Do you have a fund of skill development materials that you can recommend if several children indicate a need?

Figure (4-1)

Do's and Don'ts of Conferencing

As has been indicated earlier, there is no prescribed way to have a conference; there are only general guidelines that have been learned through many years of trial and error. Following is a list of do's and don'ts that has proved to be useful in organizing for the conference:

Do's And Don'ts of Conferencing

Do	Don't
Be you in the conference.	Try to be someone else.
Provide the stimulus.	Try to dominate the conference.
Select interesting parts (sample that which is read).	Go into detail over all that is read.
Read interesting parts orally.	Overdo it or expect the child to read anything but his best from the most exciting part of the book.
Read orally for a purpose.	Use the conference only to check on oral reading errors.
Ask open-ended questions.	Ask too many convergent questions (names, dates, places).
Not be afraid to discuss a book you haven't read.	Try to say more about the book than what you know about it.
Conference in many ways: one-to-one group with different group with same book book whole class	Underestimate the power of meeting children on a one-to-one basis.
Make a rigid conference schedule and break it.	Begin with voluntary conferences.
Ask the child to prepare for the conference.	Make light of his preparation for the conference.

Do	Don't
Take as much time as you need to conference in the beginning.	Conference more than about five minutes after you have had some practice.
Ask questions aimed at specific things.	Question just to be questioning.
Help the child make clear his responsibility.	Pitchfork him.
Have voluntary conferences.	Be too rigid about any one type of conference.
Use the conference to get clues for grouping.	Try to teach the same skills to everyone at the same time.
Make the place for conferencing as psychologically safe as possible.	Conference where you do not have privacy or can be overheard by the class.
Use the conference to both diagnose and instruct.	Use it only for diagnosis or instruction.
End the conference on a happy note.	Let the child leave without some self-evaluation and knowing his next step.
Organize the classroom in such a way so everyone knows what to do.	Tolerate interruptions.
Use the conference as a guidance function.	Talk only about books and reading skills.
Question in as realistic and honest a way as possible.	Ask canned questions.

Do	Don't
Write during the conference or immediately thereafter.	Try to save up all of your thoughts until you have finished conferences for the day.
Try to see the child every third day.	Wait too long between conferences.
Use others to help you conference (students, teacher aides, parent aides, university student teachers, etc.).	Allow people to conference who have not had some training and know the purpose of PRI.
Inquire.	Interrogate.

Figure (4-2)

80

Summary

Few things will excite and stimulate the child as much as regular conferencing with his teacher. Children seem unanimous in their love for the conference. If you don't believe that, walk into a class that has personalized reading and announce that you will be their teacher this morning and that you are going to dispense with the teacher's plans and implement your own. The first question will be: "How about the conferences . . . can we have them?"

Following are some comments children have made about conferences. Judge for yourself whether or not they should have a place in the classroom:

> "I like to go to a conference because I want to find out what the teacher thinks of my work."
>
> "I like it when you say I am doing good."
>
> "I like to read to you in private."
>
> "I like conferences because you can tell me where I am strong and where I am weak in reading."
>
> "I like to tell about my book."
>
> "I like conferences because you can learn new things."
>
> "I like conferences when you can tell your teacher what you are having trouble with."
>
> "I like conferences because my teacher gets to know what kind of books I like and she can help me find a book if I have one that is too hard or too easy."
>
> "I like conferences because I get to know my teacher better and she gets to know me."

The Conference IDEA Bank

1. Each student should keep a journal containing things they have learned while reading books, creative writings, and any other private ideas they may have. They should share this only with their permission.

2. For some reason, fraction boards and pocket charts seem to be present in abundance in almost every classroom. They have nice grooves for slipping cards in and out, a perfect way to schedule conferences.

3. If children are concerned about when they will have a conference, put all of their names on a ditto and pass them out. This will give them an idea of when they are up for a conference.

4. One of the best ways to get ready for conferencing with children is

to learn about some of the outstanding guidance programs that are available today. Seek them out; they are sure to help you become more proficient in conferencing. Some examples are:

Bessel, Harold and Uvaldo Palomares, *Human Development Program* (San Diego, California, Human Development Training Institute, 1969).

Borton, Terry, *Reach, Touch and Teach* (New York, New York, McGraw-Hill Book Company, 1970).

Glasser, William, *Schools Without Failure*, (Los Angeles, California, Educator Training Center, 1969).

Gordon, Thomas, *Parent Effectiveness Training*, (Pasadena, California, Effectiveness Training Associates, 1971).

Harris, Thomas, *I'm OK–You're OK*, (New York, New York, Harper Row Publishers, 1969).

Randolph, Norma, William Howe, and Elizabeth Achterman, *Self Enhancing Education*, (Santa Clara, California, Self Enhancing Education, Inc., 1972).

5. As you move from basal readers to self-selected books, it is good practice to conference in the basals. Simply ask the children: "Whoever finishes the story may have a conference with me if they wish."

6. Video tape your conferences in the beginning of the year. Do it again two months later and see if you have improved.

7. Ask another teacher to evaluate how you are relating to the child while conferencing.

8. Role play a conference.

9. Prior to a group conference, write out some thought-provoking questions. Ask each child to respond to those questions before coming to the conference.

10. Ask parents to visit class during conferences. After the conference is over, and the next step has been determined, meet with the parents and explain what happened. Show them their child's folder so they can be assured of accountability.

11. Visit other teachers who successfully use personalized reading. Tape some of their conferences. Analyze.

12. Following are some situations in which it is appropriate to have group conferences:

    a) When all of the books lend themselves to the same kind of questioning. (Fact, Interpretative, and Evaluative)

    b) When several children are reading the same story in a basal reader or some supplementary material.

    c) When several children have chosen a book around the same theme. (Horses, Race Cars, Mystery)

    d) When several children have chosen a book by the same author. (Laura Ingles Wilder, Beverly Clery, Dr. Suess, etc.)

    e) When several children have chosen books from a series. (*Nancy Drew, Hardy Boys, Childhood of Famous Americans,* etc.)

    f) When several children are reading books of poetry.

    g) When several children are reading fiction or non-fiction.

    h) When several children are reading books dealing with current events.

    i) When several children are reading books that help them repair or make things.

13. One of the best programs available to help teachers improve the art of questioning is the Great Books Program. It divides questions into Fact, Interpretative, and Evaluative questions and helps the teacher determine when it is appropriate to ask each. For more information write: Great Books Foundation, 307 North Michigan Avenue, Chicago, Illinois.

FOOTNOTES

[1]Jeannette Veatch, *Reading in the Elementary School* (New York, New York: Ronald Press, 1966), p. 120.

[2]Norma Randolph, William Howe, and Elizabeth Achterman, *Self Enhancing Education: A Training Manual* (Santa Clara, California: Self Enhancing Education, Inc., 1971), p. 64.

[3]Lyman Hunt, "The Key to the Conference Lies in the Questioning," (Burlington, Vermont: University of Vermont), pp. 2-6.

chapter five

Record-Keeping in Personalized Reading Instruction

It has always been important to keep records of the material which each child has read, the difficulties he has encountered and the success he has had in overcoming these difficulties, the level at which he is reading at various times during the year, and his attitude toward reading. In the basal reader program this record, which would have been so helpful to the logical development of the child's skill instruction and development of interest in reading, has been substituted with usually no more than the name of a basal reader and occasionally the page on which the student was reading. For the average child making average progress and the above-average child who was not allowed to make more than average progress, it was assumed that they completed the reader and the skills at the grade level of the past year and were now ready for the basal reader of the next grade. This may or may not have been the case, but the teacher nevertheless assumed that it was and began with most children at the basal reader of that particular grade level.

In the personalized program, however, there is no such material so that the next teacher will know where to start, unless the teacher from the year before has kept careful records and passes these along with the children, showing materials read, and skills upon which the child has worked. In the personalized program, the teacher must be able not only to remember what each of the groups is doing but also to keep careful record of what each child is doing. Only by careful record-keeping can she be sure that the child is making the expected progress, is reading a wide variety of materials, and is benefiting from the instruction itself. The importance of efficient record-keeping practices cannot be overemphasized. This is absolutely essential in the personalized program. Even though the child may keep his own record of materials read, the teacher must keep a careful record of the individual conference and what is accomplished.

The time to keep these records is either while the teacher is conferencing with the child or immediately after the conference. It is impossible to recall with any degree of certainty what was done with each child if the teacher waits too long after conference time is over. The appropriateness of when to record pertinent data is accurately said in the New York Board of Education's *A Practical Guide to Individualized Reading*:

> The teachers had their records readily accessible when working with an individual child. Sometimes the teacher made her entries in the presence of the child in order to keep him appraised of his own specific needs and assets. At other times, when the notation might prove to be a threat to the child or might resemble a testing situation too closely, the entries were made after the child had left the teacher's presence. [1]

The importance of accurate record-keeping cannot be overemphasized. To wait until more than five or ten minutes has elapsed is one of the surest ways to hasten the deterioration of the personalized reading program and, in its place, create nothing more than an independent reading program.

Essentially, the information which must be included will be the date of the conference, so that no child will miss having a conference at least once every three or four days. The name of the book which the child is reading and the page on which he is reading should be recorded. The questions he has or the difficulties he has encountered should be noted, as should any suggestions concerning the tasks to be carried out. A comprehension check rating is probably essential at each conference. Notes should be made of any skill instruction which the child needs but which the teacher feels can just as well be supplied later in a small group.

In some situations the teacher has forms with children's names and blank spaces already prepared. With the child's name at the left of the page, and a place for the date, the skills which the teacher feels are necessary at that particular age level are listed across the top of the page. In this way the teacher is reminded to check each child on these skills and provide practice and instruction in those skills with which the child needs additional help. Following on page 87 is an example of such a multi-purpose skills form.

The Child's Records

As the children are doing their individual reading, they keep a record of the book which they have read on a five by seven inch sheet of tagboard. The

Readings Skills Check List

Names	Date	Consonant Sounds	Date	Blends	Date	Consonant Digraphs	Date	Endings	Date	Vowels

Figure (5-1)

title of the book should be stated with the author's name, general reaction to the book, suggestions about the worth of the book, and the category into which it falls. The publisher, the date of publication, length of the book, and a summary are optional things that could be reported if the child and teacher desire. This type of record is recommended because it is an efficient device to determine changing interests, attitudes and growth in reading, as well as a booksharing technique which children will use to select books. Following is a sample card that could be used:

Name: _____

Title: _____

Author: _____

General Reaction to the Book: _____

_____

_____

_____

Sharing Guide: (Circle that which you think is appropriate)

Suggested reading for: Boy   Girl   Both
Recommendation: Excellent   Very Good   Good   Fair   Poor

Category of Book: autobiography   biography   sports   mystery
                          science   animals   other

Figure (5-2)

Besides the card file, each child should have a loose-leaf, three ring notebook. Whereas the card file is a public record of what each child is reading, the notebook is a private record shared only between the teacher and the child, unless of course the child wishes to share it with someone else. This notebook can be used to keep lists of various kinds of words, a daily record of the child's reading, a daily journal for writing, or a file to keep assignments or appointments. A manila envelope taped to the back cover of this notebook could also help store things such as worksheets completed, book-sharing projects to be shared, or cards to show the teacher prior to the time they are filed for the class.

At the time of the conference the child brings his notebook and any completed cards to the teacher so that the teacher may quickly check on the amount of reading that he has done, his selection of materials, the words he has been having difficulty with, and his general attitude toward reading.

The advantage of keeping this information in a notebook is that it is less easily lost. It also is a valuable aide in that pages can readily be added or deleted and the child can daily reorganize his record-keeping system as he desires. The advantage of having some material on cards is that it may be filed. As the child reads more books, the cards can then be categorized and may actually be used by other students to aid them in deciding if they want to read a particular book. Every book which a child attempts, however, whether he finishes it or not, should be recorded. Both the things that he has read and enjoyed, as well as those things which he has either started and not finished or which he has read and disliked, will become valuable information for the teacher in understanding a particular child.

If a child prepares reading cards, they should be kept either in a file which the child keeps at his desk or, if they are to be used by other children, in a file under each child's name at some place close to the table or shelf where the books are kept. They should not be allowed to be taken from the classroom. As the child prepares note cards and brings them to the teacher at the time of the individual conference, they are added to his file.

At the end of each year, before the teacher gives each child his set of cards to take home, she could distribute with them a simple form to summarize the child's reading. This form will serve as a useful device to help next year's teacher determine the child's interests and attitudes about reading. A form similar to the one on page 89 could be used.

The Teacher's Records

Teachers of personalized reading usually keep two kinds of records: those which serve day-to-day purposes and those which are a permanent record of the child's progress. Because the daily records are so vital to the teacher's ongoing diagnosis and formation of groups, the need for them is obvious. They become the heart of the teacher's attempt to find out not only where the child is but also how far the child can be taken. The need for the more permanent record is also

```
Card File Summary

Name _____ Year in School _____ Date _____

School _____ Teacher(s) _____

1. Total number of books read: _____

2. Categories:              No:                                    No:

   A. autobiography         _____      D. mystery                 _____
   B. biography             _____      E. science                 _____
   C. sports                _____      F. animals                 _____
   G. other: _____                      _____

3. Comments: _____

   _____
```

Figure (5-3)

important, but for other reasons. Whenever the teacher moves a child from the basal program to the personalized program there is the potential for misunderstanding among parents. Therefore, this permanent record is the device which insures a continuous program of skills. It is also helpful to the next teacher and it becomes a continuing record of the child's reading progress in the elementary school.

When devising a system of permanent record-keeping, it is wise to keep two things in mind: (1) the system must be rigid enough to insure its being understood by all who use it; and (2) it must be flexible enough to allow for differences among teachers as well as the changing scene which a teacher finds as she works with children day after day. Following is an example of one school's policy statement on record-keeping that was cooperatively made by principal and staff:

RECORD-KEEPING IN PERSONALIZED READING

Personalized reading is rarely discussed without debating the issue of record-keeping. Everyone agrees that record-keeping is an important aspect of personalized reading, yet no one has devised a good system.

The problem of developing a system that everyone can utilize effectively lies in the uniqueness of each teacher. However, interested as educators may be in uniqueness, there is still a need to develop a certain amount of conformity or structure in this matter of record-keeping if for no other reason than to bring a sense of sequence to the teaching of reading. It is with this in mind that we have developed the following policy statement that is rigid enough to give the program structure, yet flexible to allow for the uniqueness of each teacher using the system.

Forms in the Child's Folder

The forms in the child's folder will be of two kinds: those which must be used to give the program continuity and those which are optional.

I. *Forms that must be used:*

There are three forms which everyone must use. They are: (1) the Barbe Skills Check List; (2) the Daily Conference Data Sheet; and (3) the Permanent Record of Personalized Reading. All of them are *YELLOW* and give valuable ongoing data about the child's progress in reading. (There is no deviation from these forms. Forms can be added or deleted from this list only upon the recommendation of a majority of the staff.)

II. *Forms Which Are Optional:*

Teachers are encouraged to seek and use as many different kinds of record-keeping devices as possible. When someone finds a new one he should bring it to the office and it will be duplicated for all staff members. In the event that it becomes widely used it can be added to the list of forms which all must use. These forms will always be printed *WHITE* and will become the flexible part of the record-keeping system. At the end of the school year these should be removed from the permanent folder and information transferred to the permanent forms.

Other Considerations

1. Placing a child in personalized reading is a teacher decision.
2. Children can be placed in personalized reading or taken out of personalized reading at anytime during the school year.
3. No child can be placed in personalized reading unless the teacher keeps a permanent record of his progress similar to the stated guidelines.
4. At the end of the year it is the teacher's responsibility to bring the reading folder up-to-date and remove from it anything she considers confidential or personal.
5. After the teacher has summarized the child's reading effort for that year, the folders are bundled up and sent to the principal's office for distribution to next year's teacher.

Because this record-keeping system is developed to help the teacher better diagnose and prescribe for the child, it should always be open to change. Whenever the staff finds it unwieldy and unworkable, it should be altered.

Nothing will so quickly cause the destruction of personalized reading as a record-keeping system which confines and restricts.

The Permanent Record

At the beginning of the year, or at such time as the teacher decides to place a child in personalized reading, a manila file folder is made for each child. On one side of the folder is stapled the permanent record sheet that follows the child throughout his school life. On the other side of the folder the teacher should staple a copy of the Barbe Skills Check List of as many levels as seem to be necessary. For instance, while a child reading at grade level might only have the check list for that level, the child reading two levels below might have both of them stapled to his record. Even though it is not recommended that the teacher try to push skill teaching past the child's year in school, it is still recommended that the skills check list for one level above the child's reading level be placed in the folder just to get an idea of the next level of skills.

These folders should be placed in a bin or box and be readily accessible to the teacher. This record, together with the teacher's loose-leaf notebook, will serve as the complete system of record-keeping insofar as the teacher is concerned.

Some teachers prefer to keep the daily record sheets in the child's folder while others prefer to keep the record in the notebook. This is a matter of choice, and the teacher should take whatever shortcuts necessary to assure a record-keeping system that is as efficient as possible.

At the end of the year, the teacher removes from the permanent record folders anything considered private and personal and makes a written summary for each child. This should be a great aid to next year's teacher. The folders are then bundled up and brought to the principal's office. They are distributed to the appropriate teacher in the fall of the year prior to the opening of school.

The question always comes up about what the next year's teacher is to do with the records if the personalized method is not used. Keeping in mind that no teacher is ever forced to enter this program, the teacher should keep them and look them over because they should be of value in any reading program. Some teachers use them immediately, others use them as they place children in the program, and still others never use them and simply pass them on to the next teacher. This system should in no way become a signal for the teacher to teach the personalized program.

The Teaching of Skills

Skill instruction should not go beyond the child's actual grade placement. The goal is to move each child through the skill instruction at his own pace, neither speeding him up to get him through it more rapidly nor dragging it out

(YELLOW)

Permanent Record of Personalized Reading: (Staple in Folder)

School _____

Name _____ Teacher _____ Level in School _____
                    Teacher _____ Level in School _____
                    Teacher _____ Level in School _____

	F	W	S

Approximate
Reading Level

Reading Interests: _____

Reading Needs: _____

Reading Strengths: _____

Reading Attitudes: _____

School Year: _____
Tests: Scores: Tests: Scores:
_____
_____

Comments: _____
_____

School Year: _____
Tests: Scores: Tests: Scores:
_____
_____

Comments: _____
_____

School Year: _____
Tests: Scores: Tests: Scores:
_____
_____

Comments: _____
_____

Figure (5-4)

(YELLOW)

Daily Conference Data Sheet   Name _____

Date	Book	Pages Read	Reading Skills	Follow-Up

Figure (5-5)

while the rest of the class catches up. In the personalized program, skill instruction is geared to the child's own ability to learn. Once the child has mastered the skills at his age level, no new skill instruction is presented. Skills from previous levels are checked upon and if they have not been fully mastered, they are relearned. It is true, of course, that the brighter child will acquire some of the skills of a higher level in an incidental manner. This is not to be discouraged, but neither should the teacher in any way formally present the skills of the higher levels. Looking at the child's previous records, it is possible for the teacher to determine exactly those skills which have been presented to him as indicated by the teacher's check. In some cases it will be necessary to review or actually reteach certain of the skills, but by noting whether or not the skill has been checked, it is possible for the teacher to determine if this skill is a new one for the child or one merely to be relearned.

Barbe Skills Check List

Although the Barbe Skills Check List is presented in Chapter 7, a word is needed here. In an effort to get all of the skills for a given level on one sheet of regular-size paper, they appear crowded. Therefore, the teacher may find it necessary to reproduce them on several sheets of paper to make record-keeping more efficient. The task of pretesting each of the skills, and coming back at a later date to see if the child still retains them, will be significantly easier if the spaces between each skill are larger.

Although it is appropriate to take a given skill and teach it to a child, or the whole class, it is usually more effective to teach the skill when there is a need. The teacher will find significantly more transfer in this method. Whatever the method of skill teaching, each teacher should try to devise some method of noting when the skill has been mastered, or if reteaching is necessary.

Record-Keeping and the Conference

As the teacher is questioning the child about his book, notations are made in the Daily Conference Data Sheet. Some needs will be met during the conference, while others will be saved for group teaching at a later time. Following is an example of how these records might be used:

Teacher: Let's see, Tom, (Intermediate IV) the last time you came for conference you were reading *The Enormous Egg*. I think you were on page 138. Have you finished?

Child: Yes.

Teacher: How did it end? I know it was a story of a dinosaur egg.

Child: At the end he started to work in Washington D.C.

Teacher: Who was he?

Child: Nate Twichell.

Teacher: Was he the one who hatched the Enormous Egg? And what about the dinosaur . . . how did it end up?

Child: He stayed at the museum and every few months Nate went up to see him.

Teacher: OK. Did you like the story?

Child: Yes.

Teacher: It is kind of nice to have a change of pace from a sports story isn't it?

Child: Yes.

Teacher: I see you have another sports story today . . . *Crackerjack Halfback* by Matt Christopher. He is some author, isn't he?

Child: Yes.

Name _____ Tom S. _____

Date	Book	Pages Read	Reading Skills	Follow-up
2/20	*Crackerjack Halfback*			

Figure (5-6)

Teacher: If you could say you had a favorite sport, what would it be?

Child: Football.

Teacher: What position would you like to play?

Child: Linebacker.

Teacher: Why is that?

Child: There is a lot of things you can do when you play linebacker. You can blitz and guard a lot of people.

Teacher: Do you play football?

Child: Yes.

Teacher: I see you have read 38 pages. Who is the main character so far?

Child: Freddie.

Teacher: What is happening so far?

Child: There are these two teams, the Catfish and the Sandpipers. The Sandpipers haven't won a game in two years, and today they tied the game.

Teacher: Pretty exciting, huh?

Child: Yeh.

Teacher: What position does Freddie play?

Child: It really doesn't say so far.

Teacher: Could you tell from the title?

Child: Oh, halfback.

Teacher: Where would you like to read to me, Tom?

Child:

> *"I'd hate to spill you with a stiff-arm." Freddie tried to swallow his anger. He looked at Mert. "That's a long time, yet. Anything can happen by then."*
>
> *"I know," smiled Mert. "You can lose every game! Ha-ha! So long, Cuz! This is where I turn off!"*
>
> *Why did I have to have a cousin like him? thought Freddie. He wished he had poked Mert's chin shadow once more while he had the chance.*
>
> *He arrived home and found Mom busily vacuuming the living room rug. She was tall, and pretty even with her hair rolled up on curlers. Mom worked every day in an office and had only Saturday in which to do her housecleaning.*
>
> *She saw him walk in the door and smiled. She stepped on a lever on the vacuum cleaner, and it whirred to a stop.*
>
> *"Well!" she said. "Who won?"*
>
> *"We tied," Freddie replied. "Twenty-twenty. I'm hungry, Mom. Got anything to eat?"*

"In a minute," she said. "Get those togs off and wash up."
She frowned then. "Your uniform looks pretty clean. Didn't you
play?"

He looked away and felt himself blush. "I played some," he
mumbled, and walked to his bedroom, where he started to remove
his uniform.

She wouldn't have said that if she'd gone to the game. Hadn't
he made some long runs with the ball? Hadn't he scored that last
touchdown?

He got into his other clothes, then went into the bathroom and
washed.[2]

Name _____ Tom S. _____

Date	Book	Pages Read	Reading Skills	Follow-up
2/20	*Crackerjack Halfback*	1-38	Ignores punctuation (P) Whirred	*Group* Fluency in oral reading.

Figure (5-7)

Teacher: Is this always a problem when you play on a team . . . sometimes you get to play and at other times you have to sit on the
bench?

Child: Yes.

Teacher: There was one spot, Tom, that I wondered if you understood
what was said. "He tried to swallow his anger." What does that
mean?

Child: (long pause)

Teacher: How about if I say it is raining cats and dogs. What does that
mean?

Child: It means that it is raining real hard.

Teacher: OK, you're doing a great job with that book, Tom. Yesterday we
went to the city library and got a whole lot of new books. I think
you will be interested in many of them. Do you have any special
plans for your book?

Child: Yes, I think I am going to do a project.

Teacher: Did you find any hard words in your reading so far?

Name _____ Tom S. _____

Date	Book	Pages Read	Reading Skills	Follow-up
2/20	*Crackerjack Halfback*	1-38	Ignores punctuation (P) Whirred Figure of speech	*Group* Fluency in oral reading Do some whole class work in figure of speech

Figure (5-8)

Child: (Tom shows a list with the following words: crouched, sprawled, smeared, and vinegar.)

Teacher: The first three are really football words. Let's see if we can unlock them. What do you suppose we could do that might make unlocking these words easier?

Child: I suppose we could find out how they are used in the story.

Teacher: Right. However, I think if I give you a couple of clues you will know what they are. The first one is probably the hardest. The (cr) in this word sounds like the (cr) in crook and crank. What do you think it is?

Child: (The child says the word correctly and tells about its use in the story.)

Teacher: How about the second one. How many of the beginning letters form a blend?

Child: Two.

Teacher: Look again, Tom.

Child: Three.

Teacher: Right. The (spr) blend has the same sound as in spread and spray. Now what do you think it is?

Child: (He pronounces it and they talk about its meaning in the story.)

Teacher: The last word is not quite so easy. If I cover this much of the word, (the teacher covers "egar") and tell you the (i) is short, what would you say it is?

Child: Oh! Vinegar . . . my mom uses vinegar for making pickles.

Teacher: I am kind of puzzled that a word like vinegar appears in a book on football. Let's see if we can find it. (The teacher turns to it and finds . . . "he had pep, zip and vinegar.") What do you think it means?

Child: He was pretty tough.

Teacher: Good. Do you remember what we called words used this way?

Child: Figures of speech.

Name _____ Tom S. _____

Date	Book	Pages Read	Reading Skills	Follow-up
2/20	*Crackerjack Halfback*	1-38	Ignores punctuation (P) Whirred Figure of speech Crouched Sprawled Smeared Vinegar (fgs)	*Group* Fluency in oral reading Do some whole class work in figure of speech Bring list of football action words to next conference

Figure (5-9)

Teacher: Right. Last week we talked about beginnings on words. This week I would like to talk about endings. What is it called when you put an ending sound on a word?

Child: Suffixes.

Teacher: Good . . . What suffix is on three of the hard words you brought to conference? (He says "ed.") Can you give me two other words that have the ending ing? (He says "going" and "bringing.")

Teacher: Tom, I feel you are coming along very well. Let's summarize what we did today. First, I note a little problem with oral reading. You don't seem to honor punctuation as you should. You can expect to be called to a group for that soon. The figure of speech thing is something that is kind of fun so we will have a whole class lesson on that soon. You had some trouble with a few words, but nothing serious. I feel good about your reading skills. What do you think?

Child: I'm doing pretty good.

Teacher: OK, I'll see you in a few days. Keep reading and be thinking about a project.

Grouping from the Daily Conference Data Sheet

The key to planning for the next day lies in the records that have been kept during the conference. At the end of each day the teacher spreads out the record sheets, and whenever two or more children are found to have a similar need, a group is formed. The grouping pattern might look something like this:

2/21

Groups:

Oral reading for fluency	*Figure of speech*
Tom	whole class
Fred	
Tim	*Consonant Blends*
Sally	(sh, st, sp, sm, sw, sn)
Sue	Martha
	Kim
Individual Assignments:	Larry
Tom—Football action words	Allen
John—Contractions	
Tom—Worksheet on comprehension	*Book selection*
	Terry
	Barbara
	Jerry

Figure (5-10)

The Process in Summary

1. Decide which things can be taught in the conference and which need to be saved for group teaching.

2. Note on the Daily Conference Data Sheet those things which help form groups for the next day (strengths or weaknesses).

3. Spread out the conference sheets and make groupings around common needs or common strengths.

4. Form groups. (The child stays in the group only for as long as it takes to meet a given need.)

5. Begin the process anew each day.

Optional Record-Keeping Forms

A sound system of record-keeping will allow for individual needs of the teachers using it. Every teacher should be encouraged to seek as many short-cuts to efficient record-keeping as possible. Hopefully, there will be times when staff can meet and discuss the various techniques they are using. In the event some optional form is used widely, it should be considered as part of the permanent record-keeping system. Following are several sample forms that various teachers have found to be helpful:

A.   My Reading Record   Name _____

Title of Book Date Completed	Description of Project or Activity	Reactions (How did you feel?)	Ideas and Vocabulary Comprehension

Figure (5-11)

B. Name _____

Date	Book	Skills	Notes and Assignments

Figure (5-12)

C. Name _____

Date	Oral Reading	Comprehension	Vocabulary	Word Attack	Needs

Figure (5-13)

D.   Name _____

Date	_____	Comments

Figure (5-14)

E.   Name _____

Date	Word Analysis	Comments

Figure (5-15)

F.   Name _____

Title	Author	Date	Pages	Comments

Figure (5-16)

G. Group Work   Name _____

Related Skills	Oral Reading	Project in Progress
Dictionary	Expression	Shared Interests
Outlining	Intonation	
Skimming	Punctuation	

Figure (5-17)

H. Group Work   Name _____

Comprehension	Phonetic Analysis	Structural Analysis
Sequence	Consonants	Verb forms and endings
Details	Blends	Affixes
Word Meaning	Digraphs	Contractions
Critical Reading	Vowels	Possessives
Main Idea		Syllabication
Relationship		
Inference		
Judgement		
Evaluation		

Figure (5-18)

I.   Name _____

Reading silently with ease and comprehension.			
Reads orally with fluency and expression.			
Can select the main idea.			
Can summarize or outline a story or article.			

Forms G and H are reprinted by permission from Individualized Reading from Scholastic Book Company, Englewood Cliffs, New Jersey 07632.

I. *(continued)*

Can read critically and evaluate information.			
Uses context, phonetic, and structural clues to identify words when reading.			
Can skim and scan.			
Reacts creatively to story plots and characterizations.			
Uses reference materials efficiently.			
Improves reading speed.			

Figure (5-19)

J.

+ OK   S   strength   — needs teaching   ? not sure—try later

INDIVIDUAL CONFERENCE
Check List for Writing and Reading

Name _____

DATES							
Word Recognition							
Initial Sounds							
Endings—Rhymes							
Substitutes							
Long Vowels							
Short Vowels							
Vowels affected by R							
Digraphs							
Blends							
Oral Reading—Hold Audience							
Personal Identification							

J. *(continued)*

DATES							
Main idea understood							
Mechanics							
New Words							
Study Skills (Index)							
Tricky Details							
Any other checks needed							

Figure (5-20)

K.
MY WEEKLY READING   Name: _____

Date	Name of Book	No. of Pages Read	Activities	Evaluation of Work
Monday				
Tuesday				
Wednesday				
Thursday				
Friday				
Next Week				

Figure (5-21)

Form J is reprinted by permission from Dr. Jeannette Veatch, Professor of Education, University of Arizona, Tempe, Arizona.

L.   Name of Child _____

Dates

COMPREHENSION						
1. Word Meaning						
2. Sentence Meaning						
3. Main Idea						
4. Details						
5. Sequence						
SKILLS						
1. Word Recognition						
2. Word Analysis						
3. Vocabulary Growth						
4. Phonetic Analysis						
Initial Consonants						
Vowels						
Blends						
Phonograms						
Prefixes						
Suffixes						
5. Reading Rate						
6. Mechanics of Silent Reading						
Lip Movement						
Pointing						
ORAL READING						
1. Correct Phrasing						
2. Voice Inflection						
3. Quality of Tone						
4. Pronunciation						
5. Enunciation						
6. Skipping Words or Lines						
7. Word Substitution						
8. Addition of Words						
9. Ignores Word Errors						
10. Repetition of Words						
11. Observes Punctuation						
12. Guesses at Unknown Words						
13. Reads Smoothly						
14. Transposes Words						
LOCATING INFORMATION						
1. Parts of book						
2. Reference Materials						

L. *(continued)*

Dates

VOCABULARY GROWTH PERSONAL—SOCIAL						
1. Broadening reading						
2. Enjoys reading						

Figure (5-22)

M.

DIAGNOSIS OF READING SKILLS

Name

Disability present ✓   Disability present but improved X

No longer needs help ⊘   Strength S

Date				
1. Initial consonant sounds				
2. Short and long vowel sounds				
3. Consonant blends				
4. Consonant digraphs				
5. Blends consonant and vowel sounds smoothly				
6. Recognizes syllables				
There are as many syllables in a word as vowel sounds				
If the first vowel in a word is followed by two consonants, the syllable usually ends with the first of the two consonants				
If the first vowel in a word is followed by a single consonant, the consonant usually begins the second syllable				

M. *(continued)*

	Date				
If a word ends in "le" preceded by a consonant, the consonant usually begins the last syllable					
Prefixes and suffixes are syllabic units					
A is a syllable when at the beginning of two syllable words					
7. Accent marks					
8. Vowel rules					
Vowel in one syllable word is short					
Vowel in syllable or word ending in "e" is long					
Two vowels together, first is long, second is silent					
Controlled "r" sound					
9. Compound words					
10. Root words					
11. Prefixes and suffixes					
12. Plurals					
13. Contractions					
14. Homonyms					
15. Synonyms					
16. Antonyms					
17. Dictionary skills					

Figure (5-23)

Oral Reading

Because oral reading is an important part of the individual conference, and because it is nearly impossible for both teacher and child to have a copy of the selection, especially one that can be written on, it is necessary to have a form to record oral reading errors. In situations where it is impossible to record errors in this manner, a thin sheet of paper, or a photocopy of the pages, can be used and later transferred to the form.

The child's posture, how close he holds the book to his eyes, the word attack methods he employs, how he uses his voice, and how he phrases, are a few things teachers look for while observing oral reading. Although it is not possible to check every kind of an error, it is possible to chart the most frequent kinds of errors and comment on any others which seem to effect the child's progress in reading. Following on page 109 is a form and key that can be used to give some indication of where the child needs help with regard to his oral reading:

Summary

The keeping of good records and the reporting of the results of those records to both the child and his parents cannot be overemphasized. In fact, good record-keeping is so vital to the teacher's success that this alone has the potential either to improve the teaching of reading or to frustrate it so that no one knows where the child is functioning. This chapter has tried to give a rationale for good record-keeping, ideas to help the teacher set up a record-keeping system, and a process for accurately reporting pupil progress to both the child and his parents. Consider the following when building a record-keeping and reporting system:

* Keep it simple.
* Don't hesitate to change the system when it is no longer working.
* Keep in mind the close relationship between record-keeping and diagnosis.
* Remember that good records give clues to grouping.
* Parents have a right to know where the child is in his reading at all times.
* Records are no better than those who use them.
* Don't waste your time recording things that can be done by students.

Diagnosing Oral Reading Errors

| Name _____ Date _____ |
| Level in School _____ Approximate Reading Level _____ |

Key	Comments
/ /	
O	
R	
MP	
A	
〜〜	
IP	

Key:	Explanation
/ /	Vertical lines between words denote phrasing. A line between each word indicates a word-by-word reader
O	Circle all words that are omitted.
R	Repeats words
MP	Mispronounces words
A	Adds a word (write in word that is added)
〜〜	Hesitation
IP	Ignores Punctuation

Figure (5-24)

Record-Keeping and Reporting IDEA Bank

1. Anything that helps the teacher account for some phase of the reading program is a record-keeping device. This means charts on the wall that

keep track of books read, or a cardboard "cookie jar" that is used to hold words that children either like or have trouble unlocking.

2. Make a giant poster and put the names of every book category the class can think of on the chart. Each time a child reads a book in one of these categories he should make a check next to the category. At the end of a couple of months the class will have an idea of what children are reading. The teacher might want to use this to stimulate children to read in other areas. It could also be used as a guide for book selection for the library center.

3. Ask the children to select a "Book of the Week." This can be done by allowing them to stand before the class and "sell" their book. The book chosen is placed on a chart and each week a new book is added. At the end of the month, semester, or year, all of the books on the chart can be reviewed and perhaps the best one could be "Book of the Year." (One class did this faithfully for a whole year and E. B. White's *Charlotte's Web* was chosen as "Book of the Year." The class wrote to him and received a nice letter in return. This was used the following year to stimulate the process all over again.)

4. Make a form with the names of all class members on the left side and spaces for dates on the right. Staple this sheet in a notebook and make a check on the date of each child's conference. This will be a handy reference for finding out who is coming to conference most regularly.

5. Judge your record-keeping system by how long students stay in the same group. If in a group for longer than one week, try to analyze what is happening by reviewing your record-keeping procedures.

FOOTNOTES

[1]Marcella K. Draper, Louise H. Schwietert, and May Lazar, *A Practical Guide to Individualized Reading* (New York, New York: Board of Education, 1960), pp. 53-54.

[2]Matt Christopher, *Crackerjack Halfback* (Boston, Massachusetts: Little, Brown and Company, 1962), pp. 28-29.

chapter six

Personalized Reading and the Independent Activity Period

The very principle of the personalized reading program will require that the teacher carefully plan independent activities from which the children will benefit. Basically, the first part of the planning will involve those activities in which the remainder of the class will participate while the teacher is working with some of the children individually. It is important to realize that these activities will not be centered around the traditional three—good, average, and poor—reading groups.

Remembering what it is the teacher wants to accomplish with the reading program helps in planning the activities in which the students will engage while she is busy with the individual conferences. Grouping is used in the traditional manner for skill presentation, but the group is formed only for a specific purpose and is disbanded as soon as that single, specific purpose is accomplished.

As the children had their individual conferences, the teacher may have noted the need for specific skill instruction on the part of several of the children. Either on the day she discovers this, or perhaps several days later when she has seen all of the children, she will ask these particular children to join together into a group which will then study the needed skill together. Once the skill has been presented, the group may work on their own either with or without the teacher's individual attention. They may actually work for a while on their own and then come back as a group to allow the teacher to check on how well the skill has been learned.

Groups are also formed during the independent activity period that work to develop or improve the children's interest in reading. For example, a child may join a group of other children who have read the same book to discuss his reactions to the book, sharing with others certain parts which are particularly interesting to him either by telling about them or reading them. He might join a particular group to tell them about the book he has just read so that they will know if they want to read it. Through class planning, certain procedures can be set up which include the things he should tell about the book, how much he might read from the book, and even what things he should not tell.

Certainly, for at least part of each period when the teacher is engaged with other children, each child will read silently to himself from a book of his own choice. Upon completing a book, he will make a report of the title of the book, its author, and any other information which the class and teacher have previously decided will be helpful to the child, the teacher and to other children who might want to read the book. The usual type of book report is not considered an activity which will encourage the child to read more and should be avoided.

Other suggested activities for the remainder of the class, while the teacher is working with one student individually, include (in addition to reading silently for pleasure and group work on skills and interest) such things as: keeping individual vocabulary lists of new or difficult words found in their reading; writing assignments either for a class newspaper or for providing information for other classes about their activities; preparation of research reports to be presented to the class at some time other than during the reading period; studying the derivation of words and their many meanings; and all of the enrichment activities normally used in an enriched classroom program.

Follow-up activities can be handled in several ways. Some teachers prefer to reserve a specific part of the period for this when they do not see children individually. They can go to children at their seats, join in some of the group activities, plan with the children what they will do the following day when they are working individually, aid them in deciding what they might want to read next, check materials in and out, plan new group activities, and evaluate the activities of each child when he was working without direct teacher supervision.

The success of the teacher in planning with the children those activities in which they will engage while she is busy with individual children will perhaps be a measure of the success or failure of the personalized program. Certainly, such planning should not be any more difficult than the planning of activities for any class in the more traditional three-group ability or achievement groupings. These activities must not be all teacher-planning, for the teacher has neither the time nor the ability to adapt to the wide diversity of interests of the children. The activities should be planned with the children, perhaps using the Self Enhancing Education processes that have been delineated in chapter 2: "Organizing a Classroom for Personalized Reading Instruction."

Criteria for Judging Independent Activities

The ultimate test of all independent activities can be based upon the following question: "What can these activities teach by themselves, or with the support of auxiliary personnel, that I cannot teach or need not teach myself?" In several places of this book, emphasis has been placed upon the importance of the one-to-one conference. Reading is simply not personalized unless a large portion of the teacher's time is spent working with children individually. Therefore, it is vital that the classroom environment be so responsive in meeting children's needs that teacher intervention is necessary only part of the time.

Book-sharing and learning centers, for example, are two distinct kinds of independent activities that have much potential both to promote the love of reading and to foster creativity in children. They also have the potential to involve the child so totally that the teacher, in many cases, can let the activity teach itself. Following is a list of other criteria upon which independent activities can be judged:

1. Independent activities should be so interesting and exciting that motivation to participate in them is "built-in" for each child.

    When pupils are limited only to assignments made by the teacher, it places a great burden upon the teacher to assign and check all that has been done. This practice is so lacking in creativity, artistry, and excitement for the child that almost no learning takes place.

2. Many independent activities should be so planned that the child, either alone or with other members of the class, can work without the aid of the teacher for long periods of time.

    Many teachers have rejected individualized programs on the premise that working with a child individually is an unproductive use of their time. Children have demonstrated many times that they can work productively during the independent activity period if the activities are so constructed as to be a challenge to them.

3. Independent activities should be so constructed that parent aides, teacher aides, student teachers, and student tutors can aid the child in his learning.

    One of the reasons that teachers fail to individualize instruction is their inability to control the scene if too many things are happening at the same time. The emerging trend of parental involvement and the use of other community resource persons should add real spark and excitement to the independent activity period.

4. Independent activities should be open-ended so as to promote discovery, creativity, and originality.

Typically, children spend most their time in school in activities that tend to converge upon facts. The independent activity period should be that one time during the day when children are encouraged to experiment, risk, and think at the highest level possible. This is the time when the solution of one problem opens up several other possibilities.

5. Independent activities should supplement, and not take the place of, any other part of the curriculum.

One of the common misconceptions about independent activities is that they take the place of formal instruction. Of course, this is not the case. Activities during the independent period reinforce what has been taught in the formal part of the curriculum and go beyond what has been taught formally.

6. Independent activities should be changed often enough so as not to become too repetitive.

Children will not maintain interest in the independent activity period unless some effort is made to expose them to a steady flow of challenging ideas. Book-sharing lists and learning centers must be continually changing if interest is to be kept high over a long period of time.

7. Independent activities should be so exciting that the child wants to go beyond the immediate problem.

The goal of independent activities is not so much the completion of an activity as it is the pursuing of problems beyond the scope of the intended activity. The child who, upon playing a game at the center of interest, says, "I have found a new way to play this game," is demonstrating what is meant by going beyond the immediate problem.

8. Independent activities should be planned in such a way as to allow the child to pursue learning whenever it occurs.

More and more educators are beginning to realize that school is a concept as well as a place. Just because a teacher has 30 pupils does not mean that all 30 of them should always be within the confines of the classroom. When independent activities are going well, children will be learning in the community as well as the classroom.

9. Independent activities should provide opportunities for children to be alone when the need occurs.

Nowhere but in a classroom is a human being asked to be in such close quarters with other humans for so long a time. Many of the behavior problems that exist today are the result of the bombardment of stimuli a child finds each day in his classroom. Activities need to be structured that allow the child to escape some of this stimuli.

10. Independent activities should reinforce what has already been learned in groups.

Although open-endedness is an important consideration during the independent activity period, there are times when it is entirely appropriate to structure activities that reinforce, in a positive way, something that has been taught in a group.

11. The activities should encourage children to become more responsible for their behavior.

Teachers continue to report that discipline is the number one concern in the classroom. In fact, the fear of what children who are left to operate on their own might do is the reason why education is so sterile in so many of the nation's classrooms. Few skills are needed more in today's classroom than those which call for pupils to be in charge of themselves.

12. The activities should encourage the children to use process in solving problems.

One of the great lessons of the knowledge explosion is that man can only learn but a fraction of all that is known. The best he can do is to learn processes that, once learned, have application elsewhere. Once a child is taught process, it becomes a powerful instrument to transfer learning.

13. Activities participated in during the independent activity period must have some provision for evaluation.

A characteristic of all humans is that they want and need feedback. Upon completion of tasks during the independent activity period, it is important that each child know when he is doing well and when he is having problems. Self-checking devices, auxiliary personnel, students helping students, and a supportive teacher are all ways in which evaluation can be accomplished.

Book-Sharing

Book-sharing is just as the name implies: a book has been read that so stimulated the reader that he wants to let others know about what he has learned. He chooses from an almost unlimited list of suggested projects in an effort to catch the magic in the book and thereby stimulate others to read it.

Of course, a child does not share, at least through a formal project, every book he reads. This would be an insurmountable task which would most certainly turn the child against reading as the book report did in the past. Rather, he shares only those books which have great power to him. This usually ends up to be about one out of every six or seven books read.

The teacher of personalized reading must constantly seek out book-sharing activities from which the children can draw and must present them to the children in the most interesting manner possible. Charts on the wall, card files, a book-sharing center, and lists in notebooks have all been found successful in organizing for book-sharing.

All during the week the children make book-sharing projects. These projects hang from the ceiling, rest on the shelves, lean against the chalkboard and sit on the floor. In short, they not only highlight something about a particular book, but they also do much to provide a child-centered atmosphere in the classroom at all times. At an appointed time, usually on Friday afternoon, the children voluntarily share their projects, either with small groups or with the entire class. The children choose the method that best illustrates their projects, and the choice as to whether or not to make book-sharing competitive is left up to them.

The sharing of what one has read can be an activity that takes place during the time the teacher is working individually with a child, or it can be a planned part of the period at the end of each reading period. It is perhaps only a matter of preferences and might well be used sometimes as an entire class activity at the end of the reading period and other times as a part of the small group work. Maybe those books which would be of a reading level that anyone in the class would be able to read them, and of sufficient interest that they could be shared with the entire class, and either more difficult or of specialized interest could be shared in the small group discussion.

The teacher also has responsibilities during book-sharing. She should be reading books and be ready to share what she is reading. She should protect children who have trouble presenting before the class, give ideas about how to make book-sharing more successful, provide a constant stream of new and exciting activities, and take great care in displaying book-sharing projects of all the children around the room or school.

As an instrument for keeping children meaningfully employed while the teacher is conferencing with children or working with groups, few things can equal the excitement of book-sharing. In fact, it is one of the best methods whereby the program can be evaluated, for when book-sharing is good, reading will be good.

Ideas for Book-Sharing

Prepare a "filmstrip" to be shown by winding drawings from one cardboard cylinder to another. These cylinders can be slipped on dowel rods attached to a base or made with a cardboard box.

Make a poster advertising a book.

Prepare a story dramatization to present to another group. Hold a panel discussion with several students who have read the book. Part could talk for the book and part against the book.

Write a telegram about a book using 20 words or less. Expand this to a night letter of 75 words.

Make a mural, a rebus, a diorama, a collage, or a mobile that centers around a certain book.

Write a summary of a book the way a publisher does it. Compare what is written to the professional reviewers' work.

Write a letter to a friend telling him about the book.

Demonstrate some scientific or historical episode from the book.

Make a radio, newspaper, or TV announcement to advertise the book.

Make a cartoon depicting part of the book.

Make puppets to depict a story that has been read.

Use a bulletin board to depict a book.

Ask the teacher to read a book and share it with the students.

Write a story on the most humorous incident in the book.

Write a new ending for the book.

Broadcast a review of the book over the school intercom.

Make a book jacket for the book.

Share a summary of the book with children in primary grades.

Make a table of contents for the book if it doesn't have one.

Build something from a "how to do it" book and show the class.

Make a time line of events in the story.

Do a kit on the book.

Write a movie script or radio script for the book.

Make a class file for summaries. File them by author, title or by the children's names.

Draw a picture depicting a favorite character of the book.

Make a life-sized figure of a character in the book.

Write a poem about the book.

Dress like one of the characters in the book.

Fold a piece of paper two times so there are four squares and draw four pictures that best represent the book.

Use the P.A. system to tell the children about the book.

Write a letter to the librarian to be put in the library.

Make a model of the book out of wood, clay, etc.

Write a letter to the author.

Give a talk about how the author used interesting words.

Pantomine an interesting part of the book.

Draw a comic strip of the book.

Compare two books written by the same author.

Select a book of the week, book of the semester, book of the year.

Make a bookmark for a classmate that illustrates a character or scene from the book.

Give a summary of the book, telling what was liked and what was not liked.

If several are reading the same book, have a panel discussion.

Make a scrapbook of information suggested in the book.

If the book is a travel book, prepare a travel lecture.

Make lists of facts that have been learned from a book.

Allow the audience to ask questions about the book.

Write riddles about the book.

Prepare a monologue.

Make a miniature stage and depict part of the story with dolls, wire or pipe cleaner people, papier mache figures, plaster of Paris, metal, or plastic toys.

Organize a quiz program around a book or several books.

Show how the author used descriptive language.

Modernize a character in the book.

Learning Centers and Learning Stations

Few classroom techniques have the potential to enrich the lives of children as much as learning centers or learning stations. Used by perceptive teachers for a long time, they are only now beginning to be commonplace in most modern schools.

Because most schools have their own unique way of organizing and using centers or stations, they are not the same in every school. For the purpose of this discussion, learning centers are defined as any geographical area in or out of the classroom in which children can pursue, in an organized way, activities which both supplement and enrich the formal classroom program. Learning stations, a narrower concept, are much the same; however, a station is the center broken down into its component parts, and only a few of the components are studied at one time. For instance, a science learning center may be set up around a topic like geology. Volcanoes, rock formation, earthquakes, and fossils might all be studied at the same time. The learning station would break this up into much smaller parts, and each individual station would consider one thing and study it in depth.

Whether a teacher uses learning centers or learning stations is purely an individual matter and depends upon such things as classroom arrangement, flexibility of furniture, and the curriculum the center or station attempts to supplement. Classrooms with a lot of floor space, flexible furniture, and an average pupil-teacher ratio lend themselves well to learning centers, whereas classrooms with little floor space, inflexible furniture, and a high pupil-teacher ratio favor the stations approach.

Because learning centers require a lot of teacher time, both in their organization and administration, it will be difficult for one teacher to use more than six or seven at any one time. Stations, because of their space and time requirements, can easily be organized in such a way that fifty or sixty can be used at the same time.

It is recommended that each teacher or team of teachers decide for themselves what arrangement best meets the needs of their classroom. Space, student receptivity to individual responsibility, curriculum, and the attitude of the teachers will all play an important role in deciding which to use.

There are a lot of misconceptions about learning centers or learning stations. Some teachers feel that a child who works at a mathematics center does not receive formal mathematics instructions. Although this could happen in a classroom which uses centers or stations exclusively, it is more the exception than the rule. There are also those who feel children are not responsible enough to work at centers or stations. However, teachers using centers or stations report that discipline actually improves as a result of children being allowed to pursue learning in this manner. Thirdly, there is the misconception that there is neither time nor money to have centers or stations in the classroom. Time may be a problem; teachers will need to assess how they use their time and probably reapportion some of it. As far as money is concerned, most of the things commonly used in centers or stations are inexpensive and require very little money. All that is needed is the desire to seek out those materials and supplies that are available in many local establishments.

Why use learning centers or stations? Dr. Richard Hanson, in the March, 1971 issue of *Insights*, a publication of the Center for Teaching and Learning at the University of North Dakota, writes about the unique characteristics of children which make the use of centers or stations appropriate. He says, "Teachers using these more informal, personalized methods generally accept the following assumptions about children: (1) children are by nature curious and want to learn; (2) individual learning styles differ and, given the opportunity, children will learn best in their own fashion; (3) the basis for effective learning is firsthand experience; and (4) the basic responsibilities of the teacher include creation of an environment that is responsive to the learning needs and interests of the child and the encouragement and enrichment of each child's own learning efforts."[1]

Kinds of Learning Centers

A learning center or learning station can be organized around almost any topic and be made exciting to children. Because stations are usually set up around one small topic, they are not easy to name. Centers, however, are organized around large topics. Following is a list of some of the most common ones:

1) Library Center
2) Writing Center
3) Language Center
4) Listening Center
5) Spelling Center
6) Art Center
7) Cooking Center
8) Woodworking Center
9) Sewing Center
10) Music Center

11) Drama Center
12) Chalkboard Center
13) Noisy Center
14) Dream Center
15) Audio-Visual Center
16) Science Center (water center)
17) Social Studies Center (state center)
18) Manipulative Materials Center (block center, puzzle center, cut and paste center)
19) Community Center (stores, post offices, businesses)

Advantages of Learning Centers and Learning Stations

Learning centers and learning stations accomplish a lot of things that are difficult in the typical formal classroom setting and give children options not ordinarily found in a textbook approach. When used with personalized reading, they take the pressure off silent reading and work to relate reading to the rest of the curriculum. Centers and stations tend to personalize learning by allowing the child to interact in a more meaningful way with his peers and by stepping up interaction between children and adults in the classroom. Individual responsibility is developed. Children are allowed to learn through disciplined play and move from the concrete to the abstract in a more logical exciting way. With centers and stations there are fewer power struggles between the teacher and the class because children are pursuing what is of interest to them. Teachers are free to work with children individually or in small groups, and children are free to explore, create, and solve problems independently.

Problems with Learning Centers and Learning Stations

Although there are many misconceptions related to learning centers and learning stations that simply are not problems, there are some factors which can cause difficulty and must be overcome.

Time: Teachers must commit themselves to spending some time gathering materials and changing the activities often enough in order to present challenges to the children.

Housekeeping and Space: Centers take a lot of room and can make the room look unorganized. Teachers who feel strongly about a neat and clean room will have trouble accepting the problems related to organized housekeeping.

Discipline: Although research bears out that the more exciting the classroom, the less the problems with discipline, constant effort needs to be made by the teacher to use processes that call for the child to be in control of himself.

Content of Centers: Some teachers have felt that they can set up a center or station and use it for the entire year. Children soon lose interest if the activities do not constantly change.

Goals of Centers or Stations: Centers and stations work best when they are an integral part of the classroom program and not something the child can do when everything else is done. Again, teachers need to use the children as a resource in deciding how and when they will be used.

Record-Keeping: Children cannot be turned loose to work in a center or station without some accounting of where they have been and where they are going. A carefully thought-out plan of record-keeping is a necessity when using centers or stations.

Overcoming the Record-Keeping Problem

One of the most common problems associated with centers or stations relates to record-keeping. With so many children pursuing so many different learning opportunities, it is virtually impossible to know everything that each child is doing. How is this problem solved? First, it is neither possible nor advisable for a teacher to know everything a child is doing. There are times when learning is so open-ended that record-keeping would only serve to stifle learning.

There are, however, those activities which build one upon another. These are times when it is not only appropriate but also important that the teacher have some idea of what the child can and cannot do. Following are some techniques that can be used to account for learning in centers or at stations:

1) Use other adults such as parent aides, student tutors, and teacher aides to help children evaluate what they have done and where they are to go next.

2) Utilize job cards as often as possible. (The child does a task, and checks the appropriateness of his answers on the cards provided.)

3) Make as many activities as possible that are self-checking. (A common task in a mathematics center is to drill on the basic operations. A home-made device constructed out of an egg carton can be used by writing the basic facts in the "holes." A button is placed in the hole and the cover is closed. The student shakes the carton and opens it up. He tries to solve the problem where he finds the button. He then turns the carton over to see if the answer he gave is the same one that is on the bottom of the carton.)

4) Write out the most frequently asked questions about centers or stations and place them on charts for all to see.

5) Form buddy teams so one child can check the work of the other.

6) Keep an anecdotal record of each child's progress.

7) Keep a loose-leaf notebook on the progress of each child.

8) Ask the children to write in a notebook or keep a diary of their efforts at centers or stations.

Where to Find Materials for Independent Activities

Many teachers have rejected independent activities such as book-sharing and learning centers in favor of workbook activities because of the logistical problem of seeking, gathering, and storing the great variety of materials that are needed to carry out a successful program. This is a problem and only the enthusiastic teacher will take the time necessary to gather everything needed to give the independent activity period variety, excitement and creativity. Following is a list of sources from which materials for the independent activity period can be obtained:

1) Lumber Yards
2) Supermarkets
3) Contractors
4) Factories
5) Homes (Grandparents)
6) The PTA
7) The Radio
8) Rummage Sales
9) Room Projects
10) Free Materials Catalogs
11) Classroom or School Projects
12) Junk Yards
13) Clothing Stores, Paint Stores, Variety Stores
14) Repair Shops
15) Bookstores

Some teachers spend a great deal of time, especially at the beginning of the year, preparing the community for the type of program that will be in operation. They talk to businessmen about saving such things as dividers, display racks, and any merchandise that does not sell and is ordinarily thrown away. Some have even gone so far as to bring to a store a large box with their name on it. At intervals throughout the year they simply make their rounds and check to see if there is anything in the box. This is an excellent way to indicate to the store manager an interest in the things that would typically be discarded.

A Word About Using Centers and Stations

There is no best way to use either learning centers or learning stations; there are only some basic guidelines. While some teachers prefer to structure their entire day around centers and stations, others use them only to supplement and enrich the rest of the curriculum. Some prefer very specific guidelines for children working at centers, while others allow the children to work in them in a much more flexible manner. If used within the framework of personalized reading, centers, stations, or any other kinds of independent activity should support and supplement all other facets of the personalized program and not simply be used in an unstructured way. It is usually best first to consider the goals of the program and then use these independent activities to help achieve those goals. Following are a few guidelines that may help independent activities, especially centers and stations, be more successful in the classroom:

1) The teacher should begin on a small scale and add centers or stations only after the ones in operation are working well. One well-organized center or station is worth many that are poorly organized.

2) The teacher, in cooperation with the children, should decide upon the stable limits.

3) Everyone in the classroom must help make centers or stations successful by keeping them neat, replenishing them when they run out of materials, and repairing things that need repairing.

4) Each child should be committed to a plan of evaluation. Nothing will sabotage centers or learning stations as much as a group of children who know that nothing they are doing will be evaluated.

5) The teacher should use processes with the children that call for them to be responsible for self.

6) Teachers should not feel as though centers and stations must be a part of the curriculum every day, all year long. Like anything else, interest will fluctuate.

7) It is important to involve as many resource people as possible.

Evaluating the Independent Activity Period

At the end of each day, or at least at the end of the week, some time should be taken to evaluate what has taken place during the independent activity period. A good way to begin getting feedback from the children is to ask the questions: "What about the independent activity period gave you a good feeling?" and "What about the independent activity period gave you concerns?" Other questions related to this might be: (1) "What did you do during the independent activity period?" (2) "With whom did you work?" (3) "What do you plan to do tomorrow?" (4) "What could I do to make the independent activity period better?" (5) "May I see some of the work you have been doing?" or (6) "What did you learn today that you didn't know yesterday?"

Asking children for feedback about the independent activity period is very important because it creates a cohesive bond between the children and the teacher and lets the child know that his teacher wants it to be an exciting and stimulating experience. When asking the children about their experiences during the independent activity period, the teacher will find that their concerns will probably fall into three categories: (1) student discipline, (2) planning, and (3) development of individual responsibility. It will not be uncommon to hear the following statements from the children: "There were only supposed to be five people at the reading center, and there were seven there today." "Whenever Bill thinks you are not watching, he acts up." "The activities haven't been changed for a while; I've done all of them." "The activities are too easy." "The activities are too hard." "I needed red paint for my project and couldn't find any." "I just can't seem to concentrate when I am not in a group with the teacher." "I couldn't find a quiet place to work."

It is the wise teacher who calls for feedback from the children and uses them as unique resources in the problem-solving process. As the children become actively involved in this process, behavior and individual responsibility will begin to improve during the independent activity period. When a problem arises that is impeding the progress of the children, the teacher could use the following process to solve it:

Teacher: Boys and girls, I think I hear a great deal of concern about the noise level during center time. Is that correct?

Class: Yes!

Teacher: Well, I also have a concern. It gets pretty frustrating to plan all of these activities and then see some of you creating a disturbance. I am wondering what this behavior is telling me. Are you saying that you are having trouble handling this part of the day and that I should take control for a while?

Class: (Most classes, upon seeing that freedom is being taken away, will automatically say NO!)

Teacher: What do you think we can do to have a better day tomorrow?

Class: (Mary) "I think we should listen more carefully during the morning planning time."

(Fred) "I think those who can't handle the center time should have it taken away from them."

(Sally) "I think we need to help each other a little more. When we see someone having trouble, why not ask them if we can help?"

(Dick) "I think our little talk this morning will help. I think we should try it for a few more days and see if there is any improvement. If things go well, we won't need to take any action. If things go badly tomorrow, I think we should have some of these privileges taken away from us."

Teacher: You seem to be saying that you want to give it a try for a few more days without any action on my part. And if that doesn't work, you want me to be more controlling. That sounds fine to me. How about if we try it for three days and then have another session to evaluate our progress?

Summary

For too long, many of the nation's children have been exposed to an independent activity period that has done little but control behavior. The typical child meets his teacher for a reading class and this is followed by long periods of independent paper-pencil activities. At times the problem is even compounded when the child who finishes his worksheets early is asked to color them.

This should not happen in the model we have described. The child should be exposed to enough open-ended activities that are of interest to him to keep him adequately challenged for long periods of time. An extensive IDEA bank follows which should be helpful in making the independent activity period more meaningful.

Independent Activity Period IDEA Bank

One of the most difficult problems surrounding the use of centers is that of finding appropriate activities. Although activities do abound in great numbers, there is no one source available which helps teachers quickly find what they need. The purpose of this section is to consolidate enough ideas so busy teachers will not have to spend exorbitant amounts of time seeking that which they need to make centers successful.

The number of centers which could be set up in a classroom is almost unlimited. What follows is a delineation of several common ones, and many ideas for their use. In some cases actual ideas or games have been described, while in others the nature of the center, and the amount of space allotted here, dictates a rather general description of ideas.

Language Development Centers

Center: **Reading Skills Center**

Purpose: To supplement and enrich the child's reading skills.

Materials:

dictionaries	basal readers vocabulary cards
reading games	homemade word cards
reading kits	key vocabulary cards
crossword puzzles	telephone directory
catalogs	linguistic blocks
filmstrips, tapes, records, etc.	acetate sheets and marking pencils
flannelboard stories	magnetic boards and accompanying
pocket charts	materials
	assorted pictures

Activities:

Two circles, one smaller than the other, are fastened together through their centers in order to rotate freely. The centers may be fastened by a large brass fastener. Initial consonants are printed on the large circle so that different words can be formed. By rotating the larger circle initial consonants can be combined with the same phonogram. This device can be used to stress initial sounds, common phonograms, final sounds, etc.

Deal four or more cards to each child in the game. The first child reads a word. All the others who have cards with that vowel sound give this card to the first child. The game ends when one child runs out of cards.

Three cards are dealt out on which are printed syllables. Each player draws and discards until he can make a three syllable word.

Make an obstacle course on a piece of tagboard. On the course have rewards as well as penalties. One child throws the dice. He moves the number of times indicated by the dice. If he lands on certain spaces, he is required to choose a card. The cards are made of multi-syllable words. He can move as many spaces as there are syllables in the word providing he knows how many syllables there are. If he is caught moving the incorrect number of spaces, his partner can ask him to begin over.

There are two decks of cards; one of root words and one of suffixes. The child draws a card from each pile. If he can make a word he gets to keep it.

If he cannot, he places the cards back in the pile. The winner is the child having the most pairs.

The teacher makes 24 small cards. On each of these cards are placed pairs of words that are sometimes confused. The cards are distributed; each player receives one card. The first player lays down his card in front of him and reads the two words. He then must give one sentence in which the two words are used. If he does this, he keeps the card in front of him. If he cannot do this, he puts the card at the bottom of the pile, and the second player has a chance to give orally his sentence. Cards are drawn from the pile as the game progresses. The game continues until all the cards are on the table. The player with the most cards is the winner.

Children sort out word cards and put them into boxes that are marked short or long vowels, blends, etc. The player with the most correct responses is the winner.

As new words are learned, they are placed on cards. Later, small numbers can be placed in the corner of the card. Make a large wheel out of cardboard. Let the children spin the dial. The number the dial stops on is the word he must read. Have several words with the same number. If he gets the word or words right, he scores the number of points on the card in the lower right-hand corner. As the words get harder, they are given more points. The highest number of points that can be gotten is four. The highest point total wins.

Make ten one, two, and three syllable words on cards. Ask the children to sort them out. The first one to get them all correct is the winner.

Make several sets of long and short vowel signs for each vowel. ($\bar{A}\ \bar{E}\ \bar{I}\ \bar{O}\ \bar{U}$ and $\breve{A}\ \breve{E}\ \breve{I}\ \breve{O}\ \breve{U}$). Make a deck of words using each vowel sound. Shuffle the cards. Give each player a set of cards. At a given signal each student tries to get as many words under the right vowel sound as he can.

Make scrambled words on cards. See how fast the students can make words out of them.

The leader puts a long list of words on the board. The leader chooses a word and says: "I am thinking of a word that _____. "This is a good game because the leader can use every reading skill he wishes. Examples would be: (a word that begins like _____ , a word that has the blend _____ , vowels or vowel combinations, endings, prefixes, suffixes, a word that rhymes with _____ , a word that is a synonym to _____ , etc.)

Write an adjective on each of many word cards. Line them up on the chalkboard. Then write a noun or something that can be described by the words on the board. When the child has finished selecting the descriptive words, have him read them to you or members of the group to see if they agree.

Make 40 cards, each containing a one-syllable word. There must be at least two cards with the same vowel sound. Deal four cards to each player and place the rest face down in a pile in the middle of the table. The first player reads clearly any of his cards aloud. Any player who has a card with the same vowel sound pronounces his word and the first player must give him his card. The second player then lays these two cards in front of him. The first player draws a card from the pile to replace the card he has lost. The next player calls his card. If no one has a card with the same vowel sound, the next player calls a card. The player with the most cards in front of him is the winner.

Ten or more sections are marked off on a path. Two players each take a space capsule and set of cards rhyming with those on the path. The first player reads his first word aloud. If it rhymes with the first word on the path, he moves his capsule to the first place. If it is not the same, he may not move. He places the card at the bottom of the pack and the next player takes a turn.

Cut a circle out of posterboard and paste on it several pictures, each with a different beginning sound, ending, vowel sounds, etc. Make a spinner out of a brad and a paper clip and put it in the center. Then make up a series of pictures, many with the same beginning sounds and paste them on the tag. The children spin and say the name to which the spinner points. Then they select a picture which begins with the same sound.

Take a very colorful paragraph from a book. Replace some of the descriptive words with ordinary words and underline them. Have the pupils substitute these words with more effective words.

On strips of paper write compound words. Cut the words in half and place them in a box. The children try to put the words together again.

Center: **Spelling Skills Center**

Purpose: To support and supplement the formal spelling program and to move some of the reading skills to a more appropriate place in the curriculum.

Materials:

dictionaries
materials for making games, such as pizza disks, spinners, paper clips, laminating paper, etc.
thesaurus
dictionary of synonyms, antonyms, and homonyms
homemade and commercial spelling kits
magic slates
chalkboards
audiovisual equipment for taping and playback of words
key words packets

Activities:

Ask the children to:
>Read a story and find action words for a spelling test.
>Read a story and find the nouns for a spelling test.
>Make a list of rhyming words.
>Make a list of words with the same vowel sound.
>Make a list of sounds you hear in nature.
>Make a list of tastes.
>Make a list of sounds like rain.
>Make a list of smells.

Using the newspaper or news stories on television, make a list of words that are prominent in the news. Discuss the words and use them for spelling games. Emphasize meaning, usage, and etymology of the word.

Discuss the meaning of *categories*. When the pupils have paper and pencils ready, announce a specific category. Examples could be animals, space, states, words with prefixes, root word part, etc. See how many words they can write under each category.

The first player on one team spells a word. Then the first player of the second team spells a word beginning with the last letter of that word. The second team player must then spell a "chain word."

Each child in the group should have his own box with alphabetized dividers. Words are selected both by the teacher and through the child's own language. About five words per day is all that should be presented if this is used with children who have difficulty in spelling. The teacher writes a word on a three by six inch card and asks the child to pronounce it. The child spells it for the teacher. The child is given a card and writes the word four times kinesthetically with his finger. The child then turns the card over and writes the word with his pencil. The teacher checks the card and the child files it. Review the words at the end of the period. At the end of the week select five of the words for a spelling test. These words can be used for stories, study of prefixes, suffixes, root words, and many other kinds of phonetic analysis.

Make several three or four word crossword puzzles for the children to solve. Make certain the words spell vertically and horizontally.

Write each letter of the alphabet on a piece of tagboard. Place all the letters in a box. From this box have each pupil draw out seven letters without looking at them. Each pupil should use as many of the letters he drew to make a word.

Put a list of words on the board with their letters scrambled. The pupils must unscrabble the words orally, at the board or on paper.

Using the spelling list, find as many of the words as you can in a newspaper article.

Center: **Writing**

Purpose: To have an outlet for creative writing as well as a place where
children can improve mechanics in writing.

Materials:

all sorts of paper; quality and sizes
typewriter
pencils, pens, chalk, crayons
thesaurus
poetry box
box of newspaper headlines
mounted pictures
poem starters
dictionaries, pictionaries
post cards
stationary
book jackets
scrapbook
class diary
private diaries
magic slates
objects to write about
tapes from which to write (sounds, stories, etc.)
food cartons, commercials, advertisements, cereal boxes
experience charts
puppets

Activities:

Mount pictures on manila folders. On the inside of the folders facing the
picture print words that can be used to make a story about the picture.

Imagine what it is like to walk on the moon. Write a story about it and send
it to an astronaut. Ask them if your perception is correct.

Write a cinquain. The pattern for a cinquain is as follows:

	Example
First line—one word—giving title	Autumn
Second line—two words—describing title	Leaves turn
Third line—three words—expressing action	Float to earth
Fourth line—four words—expressing a feeling	And leave summer behind
Fifth line—one word—a synonym for a title	Fall

Write a limerick using words from your spelling list. The pattern for a
limerick is A-A-B-B-A-. (The first and second lines rhyme—lines three
and four rhyme and line five rhymes with line one and two.)

Write a couplet poem. An example would be: Black cat,
                                                Sat, sat.
                                                On mat,
                                                Poor cat!

Listen to an unfinished tape recorded story and make up an ending.

Provide a picture for each student or have each student bring his own. Write a creative story from the picture. Exchange stories and read.

Write letters to parents, ill classmates, grandparents, etc. telling them about the activities in school.

Write a story that ends like this:
    A. Then I woke up.
    B. He will never be forgotten.
    C. Everyone can come out now.
    D. This made John the happiest boy in town.
    E. Some guys have all the luck.
    F. I'll never do that again.
    G. I am glad you won this time.
    H. They have been the best of friends ever since.

A pun is the humorous use of a word in a way that suggests two meanings. Write as many as you can. An example is: "I'll see if I can dig something up for you," said the gravedigger.

Write a story around one of the following titles:
    A. Santa Claus   G. I Couldn't Believe My Eyes
    B. My Secret   H. Outer Space
    C. Apollo to the Moon   I. This Was My Lucky Day
    D. I Wonder   J. Was I Embarrassed
    E. Night Gallery   K. My First Camping Trip
    F. My One Wish   L. How About Me?
                                  M. Who Am I?

Write an autobiography.

Write as many words as you can think of that have recently been added to our language. Write as many words as you can think of that have been dropped because of disuse.

Trace the derivation of a word.

Make a chart for the *word of the week*. Each week add to the list. At the end of a certain period of time, use these words for writing a story.

Use one of the following incomplete sentences to make a story:
    If I had a million dollars I _____
    One dark night _____

Last night I dreamed _____
I'm not really me, I'm _____
To me school is _____
My parents _____
Love is _____
I feel sad when _____

Write a paragraph to support or contradict a common saying. Some are:
A. Look before you leap.
B. A rolling stone gathers no moss.
C. Still water runs deep.
D. Haste makes waste.
E. The early bird gets the worm.

Interpret the following figurative language:
A. Hit the nail on   E. The wind-swept prairie.
   the head.   F. Put your foot down.
B. Ride herd.   G. He is a gem.
C. I am all thumbs.   H. Bring home the bacon.
D. You are a   I. Grows like a weed.
   sparkplug.

Write a story about a dream you have had.

Clip a bunch of headlines from newspapers. Ask the children to draw one out and write about it.

Put the following question on a card: "Who do you know who would like to receive a letter from you?" Write that person a letter.

Make one envelope for each of the five parts of the story:
A. main character   D. the problem
B. character traits   E. what happens
C. scene or setting

Have the pupils suggest what will be written on the slips to go into each envelope. The slips in the first envelope will have on them suggestions for the main character in the story the children will write. The slips in the second envelope will have suggestions for the character trait of the main character. For example, the child may draw from the first envelope a slip with *a child of eight* printed on it: this would be the main character for his story. A slip would be drawn from each envelope to get the component parts of his story.

Write a haiku. Haiku is a kind of Japanese poetry. It often describes one of the seasons of the year or expresses a very special feeling. Haiku has only three lines. The first line has five syllables, the second line has seven syllables, and the third line has five syllables. It does not need to rhyme. The emphasis should be upon one thought expressing a feeling. Example:

> After the bells hummed
> and were silent, flowers chimed
> a peal of fragrance

Give the children a cartoon or funny strip with the captions cut off. Have them write a conversation or caption which fits the action.

Ask each child to keep a journal. This is a special folder where children can write exactly how they feel. The teacher never looks in the journal unless the child wants to share his writings.

Ask the children to finish these sentences:

    I would like to see _____
    I would like to hear _____
    I would like to feel _____
    I would like to smell _____
    I would like to go _____

Write a language experience story by writing a beginning sentence on the chalkboard. The class chooses among the sentences suggested by class members and the story is completed. The story can be read back, analyzed for structure, or cut up and put back together.

Take a sheet of typing paper and tear a design in the middle of it. After you have finished, decide what your design looks like. Then add things like arms, legs, wheels, horns, etc. to make it even more realistic. Write a story about the picture.

To increase quantity in writing use the following ideas: Make writing competitive by selecting partners. Set a timer for ten minutes. Ask the students to write as much as they can during that time. If they run out of ideas they should continue to write anything that comes to mind. A variation of that would be to continue writing the last word or last line until ideas begin to flow again.

Center: **Mathematics**

Purpose: To allow children to develop thinking processes as a result of manipulating the tools of mathematics and to supplement and enrich formal mathematics instruction.

Materials:

play money	chalkboards
attribute blocks, people pieces	ruler, yardsticks
measuring devices	worksheets in laminated covers
blocks, heads, etc. for counting and classifying	magic slates
	many math books
games and puzzles	dominoes
counting frames	hundreds chart

fraction boards	commercial charts
cuisenaire rods	flashcards
number lines	geoboards
clocks	pegboards
magnetic board and accompany- ing materials	thermometers
	metric devices
dice	tapes and records
compass, protractors	abacus
geometric shapes	flannelboard cutouts
feltboard	menus

Activities:

Use any of the four basic operations to make up problems. Write the problems in the holes of egg cartons. Put a button in one hole. Close the container and shake. Open the carton and give the answer to the problem with the button on it. Look on the back and see if you are correct.

Make a four lane race track and divide it into sixteenths. Label 1/8, 1/4, 3/8, 1/2, 5/8, 3/4, and 7/8 for each inch. Make a spinner board with all fractions on it. Also make divisions on the spinner board entitled: Take An Extra Turn, Go Back Home, and Lose One Turn. Each child spins the spinner and moves as many spaces as indicated on the board. The first child to the end of the track is the winner.

Cut a piece of board two inches wide and seven inches long. Make nine holes equal distance apart. Place four white golf tees on one side and four red golf tees on the other side. The object of the game is to interchange the white tees and the red tees. The following rules apply: 1. The white tees must all move one way and the red ones the other. 2. You can move only one tee at a time. 3. You can move to an adjacent hole. 4. You can jump, but only one tee of the opposite color. (If the children are having trouble with this game use fewer tees.)

Cut a piece of board two inches wide and six inches long. Place three pegs on the board equal distance apart. Place five metal washers on the middle peg, each slightly smaller than the next. Transfer the washers from the center peg to either of the other pegs, ending with the washers arranged in the same order as at the start. You may move only one washer at a time and a larger washer may never be placed on top of a smaller one.

Make a set of job cards on mathematical terms. Put the questions on one side of the card and the answers on the other.

Obtain commercial kits that help the children build computational skills.

Make tapes on the basic operations.

Display posters around the center that chart progress in computational skills, problem solving, etc.

Run off several copies of duplicating masters. Place in file folders and mark them in such a way a child can work independently.

Make crossword puzzles on the basic operations.

Have some programmed mathematics book available for children who wish and/or need enrichment in some area of mathematics.

Two concentric circles are drawn on the chalkboard about one foot apart, with the diameter of the inner circle about one foot in length, making the diameter of the outer circle three feet. Number combinations are written around the track. The first player shakes a dice and moves the number indicated. He then solves the problem. If correct, he stays where he is. If not, he must start over.

Draw a circle on the chalkboard. You will need as many circles as there are teams. The circles should have numbers written around the edge only. The number in the center, or the multiplier, is written in later. Numbers are put in different order around the circle. Multipliers may be varied to meet the needs of each child playing the game. A pupil from each team goes to the board and faces the group. The teacher writes in the multipliers. At a given signal, the pupils face the board and write the product beside the outside numbers. After one minute the students stop. The answers are erased after they are corrected and new multipliers are used.

Place ten or more flashcards on the chalkboard. At a given signal, the child is asked to write the answers above the combinations.

Set up a play store.

Make up several problems on menu math.

Give each child $1,000 for investment in the stock market.

Give each child a pretend sum of money to plan a camping trip in the mountains. Ask him several questions that require computation.

Make up a set of cards with mathematics symbols on them. Make another set of cards with the answers written out. Ask the children to match them.

Put addition or subtraction facts on a checkerboard. The game is played as usual except the child is asked to give the combination as soon as he moves to a different space.

Make two discs with spinners. Many games can be played by placing various combinations of numbers or symbols on the two discs.

Make up some problems on road maps.

Make up some problems using charts and graphs.

Make a ladder out of poster paper. Make up a set of combinations and place them on the rungs of the ladder. The child climbs the ladder if he continues to answer the problems correctly.

Take two five x 12 inch pieces of tagboard and fasten them together with both ends open. Make a slide slightly smaller with number combinations on them. Put the answers for each combination directly behind them. Cut a window on the front and back so you can self-check as soon as you solve the problem.

Make a ditto with a small circle in the middle. Put a fraction in this space. On the outside of the circle place several other fractions. The child closes his eyes and puts his pencil on the paper. He then adds, subtracts, multiplies, or divides this fraction with the one in the circle.

Make a chart with 36 squares. One square is the starting place and arrows are drawn through each square with *HOME* as the finishing spot. Put a numeral in each square. Make up a packet of cards. The child chooses a card and divides that number by the first one on the chart. He may move as many places as there is a remainder.

On four pieces of tagboard write: Whole Numbers, Mixed Numbers, Improper Fractions, and Proper Fractions. Then make ten cards for each of them. (Example: 6, 1-1/2, 9/7, 1/2). The child is to see how fast he can put the cards under the proper heading.

Center: **Social Studies**

Purpose: To supplement and enrich social studies teaching and to teach children about the human group.

Materials:

newspapers	travel brochures
atlases, encyclopedias, globes	magazines
maps	*Weekly Reader* and *Junior Scholastic*
pictures	
tapes	news items (local, state, and national)
records	
materials acquired from free materials catalogs	various textbooks
	listening center
scrapbooks	ethnic kits
commercial and homemade kits	simulation games
materials to make shadow boxes, and models	

Activities:

Set up a station in the center for newspaper study.

Draw a symbol of patriotism and write a paragraph on ways it can be demonstrated.

Study the history of the American flag.

Make a set of cards which ask the child to match pictures or definitions with each of the social sciences.

The Thematic Approach to social studies is an attempt to select a theme that is so powerful that the children will want to study it in depth, and this in-depth study will cause them to pursue related topics. Fill the center with all sorts of artifacts that have the potential to create great interest. Some examples are: arrowheads, bottles, bones, and antiques. The child selects the artifact of his choice and begins to study it. For instance, someone might bring a set of tongs that belonged to the sawmills of the 1800's. He might first study lumbering as it was then. This might be followed by a study of how lumber was prepared for processing. He might then become interested in the lumberjack (where he came from in the old country, etc.), and before long, the child has moved away from the central theme. As he studies these interesting topics, he then tries to relate all of them to the central theme.

Make a set of cards on science-related topics such as rain, climate, weather, etc. Try to build the understanding that the environment has a terrific impact upon man.

Make a shadow box of something of interest about a country or its peoples (dress, education, geography, family life, food, etc.).

Make a scrapbook of current events (local, state, or national).

Write a theme entitled, "Humans Are More Alike Than Different."

Make a slide-tape presentation of: (1) your city; (2) your state; or (3) a community resource person.

Make up a set of outline maps for use in the center. They could be covered with acetate for maximum use.

Make a station on ecology, pollution, poverty, etc. (Make a set of debate cards.)

Use some of the many commercial kits or simulation games in your center.

Invite foreigners to come in and talk about their country. Tape what they say for playback in the center.

Make up a packet on citizenship responsibilities such as voting, participating in community discussions, debates, projects, etc.

Write up some guidelines for writing letters to famous people.

Tape significant things from the television for playback later in the center.

Write an advertisement that would make tourists want to come to your town or state.

Do a project on the significance of holidays.

Make some crossword puzzles on important topics in the social studies.

Encourage children to travel with their parents. When they get back ask them a set of questions related to their travels.

Make a set of learning experiences on *how to*. (How to make: steel, textiles, glass, paper, etc.)

Make up a set of job cards on the effect climate, values, and religion have upon how different people dress.

Make up cards on how a bill becomes a law.

Make copies of the great documents, important speeches of the past, and put them in the center. Ask the children to memorize parts of them, do pantomines, or in someway better grasp their significance.

Make a set of experiences to better help children understand the legislative, executive, and judicial branches of our government.

Prepare some worksheets on farming, lumbering, industry, or religion for the various cultures that are being studied.

Cut out all of the pictures you can find on various aspects of human affairs. They can be used in all sorts of ways to better understand other cultures.

Put pictures in the center that have great emotional impact. Ask the children to write about them.

Have a project that helps children identify with the people of the world.

Have a list of pen pals.

Make a set of cards based on "Why" questions. (Why do people wear what they wear?, use this type of transportation?, look so sad?, etc.)

One of the best sources on careers is the *Yellow Pages of Learning Resources*, available through the National Association of Elementary School Principals. (1801 North Moore, Arlington, Virginia) This fine book lists many center activities related to community helpers, careers, etc.

You have just been given $1,000 and a two week vacation. How would you get the most out of the money? Where would you go? What would you buy? What would you see?

Make a set of our state cards.

Find art prints of some of the great historical events in the history of the world. Ask the children to report on them.

Make out an incomplete sentence exercise asking some questions that have implications for social studies. For instance, if the class is studying Viet Nam, you could get at many feelings by asking such questions as: If I were . . . I feel . . . Our country . . .

Learn a native dance and teach it to someone.

Purchase social studies games, puzzles, and simulations for the center.

Make a set of pictures of great Americans and ask questions about them.

Paste great sayings of famous people on tagboard. Ask the children to memorize them, use them in stories, or tell about the significance of them.

Make a set of cards on sign language. Use it to communicate with each other.

Study various monetary systems. Ask the children to bring in coins of other countries.

Make a set of experiences on values clarification. Use Sidney Simon's book, *Values Clarification; a Handbook of Practical Strategies For Teachers and Students*. (Hart Publishing Co., New York, N.Y.)

Go through several social studies texts and cut out all of the pictures. Place them in a box in the center. Ask the children to dip into the box and draw one out. They should then write something significant about the picture.

Make a time line for the center. Ask the children to sequence pictures, events, wars, speeches, or great human events, along the line.

Find pictures of all state flags. Match them with the state and give the significance of the symbol.

Most social studies texts have glossaries. Copy the words on a three by five card with the definitions on the back.

Social studies books are filled with charts and graphs. Cut them out and place them in acetate. Ask questions about them.

Center: **Art**

Purpose: To enrich and supplement the book-sharing portion of reading instruction and to provide an open-ended experience for children which will afford them another avenue of expression.

Materials:

easels
paint brushes
all sizes, kinds, and textures of paper
paints (finger, tempera, water, oil), chalk, charcoal, marking pen, crayons, glue, paste, starch, wheat paste
smocks and protection coverings
cans and bottles of all kinds
clay, plaster of Paris
paint chips, wallpaper samples, yarn, paper scraps, burlap materials, pipe cleaners, wire

magazines and catalogs
books on arts and crafts, painting, art objects, prints
materials for woodcarving and sculpturing
brayers and rollers
modeling tools
sandpaper

Activities:

Make a puppet face of an animal or human from a paper bag. Be as creative as you can with string, buttons, chalk, and paper scraps.

Pour a small amount of buttermilk on a piece of drawing paper. Draw on it with colored chalk.

Make a mobile out of wire or twigs. Hang homemade book jackets from them and display around the center.

Make a potato print.

Take a sheet of construction paper. Tear a hole in it and make a drawing around the hole. The same thing can be done with a blot of paint.

Make a design out of toothpicks, cereal, grain, candy, etc.

Find a picture in a magazine. Cut it in half and draw the other half.

Make animals out of pipe cleaners.

Make something out of plaster of Paris and paint it.

Cover a blown up balloon with strips of wet newspaper and wheat paste. Use several layers and finish the top layer in white smooth paper. After the papier mache has dried, pop the balloon. Paint the shell in various colors and add anything you wish to make various kinds of faces.

Cover various shaped bottles with pictures. Shellac them after they dry.

Make greeting cards with scraps found in the center.

Make a relief out of soft wood, cardboard, or styrofoam, and paint it.

Make a shield on heavy cardboard and paint it.

Make a model out of clay based upon how you feel at the time. Write a paragraph about it.

Make a collage and tell about it. (magazine pictures, buttons, string, yarn, bottle caps, etc.)

Make a picture using finger painting.

Spread a thin layer of paint over a piece of heavy cardboard. Lay a sheet of paper on top of the paint area and draw on the paper with a sharp object, pressing the lines into the paint. Pull the paper back to expose your pencil drawing.

Make a sculpture out of toothpicks, egg cartons, thread spools, or boxes. Paint it when finished.

Make a totem pole by stuffing paper bags with newspaper. Insert cardboard tubes through the bags in such a way that part of the tube sticks out. Put faces on each of the bags with paint, yarn or any other scraps that happen to be around the center. Fasten a pole in a bucket of sand and place all of the finished heads on the pole.

Put a paper cutout on a piece of colored burlap and stitch around the cutout with some brightly colored yarn. Tear the paper off and the outline will be left.

Take one teaspoon of India ink and drop it in the center of a piece of paper. Then blow through a straw to get various lines and shapes. Add various colors to make the design more attractive.

Place drops of tempera of one or more colors on the paper. Fold and press the paper so the paint will be squeezed and blotted. Cut out the dried designs and mount them in such a way as to show a colorful picture.

Make a mural on a long sheet of butcher paper.

Paint a monster on a piece of regular paper with tempera paint or on finger painting paper with finger paint.

Draw a design or picture with crayons. Cover the crayon drawing with tempera paint or paint lines and shapes over the crayon pictures.

Paint a picture or make a design using small pieces of sponge.

Wash a large, smooth stone. Paint the stone and finish it with shellac.

Set up a station in the center where some individuals can do oil painting.

Place a large sheet of butcher paper in the center and invite anyone who wishes to make some kind of a drawing.

Place wax paper over a sheet of drawing paper. Draw on the wax paper with a pencil or something hard. The pressure of this object will cause the design to adhere to the drawing paper. Remove the wax paper and brush over the drawing paper with water color. The wax lines with remain white.

Make a picture with several hidden pictures in it on a ditto. Make several copies and leave in the center. See if the other children can find the hidden pictures.

Have a classmate stand in front of an opaque projector and draw his portrait. Fill in features to make the picture look more realistic.

Make up some job cards describing some weird looking monster. Ask the child to make a drawing of what he perceives.

Use a compass, protractor, or circular object to make designs on a piece of paper. Color each of the designs a different color.

Lie down on a sheet of butcher paper and have a classmate draw around you. Fill in clothing and facial expression with the media you choose.

Make a design with tempera paint and sprinkle salt on the paint while it is still wet. Shake off the excess salt when the design is dry. The finished product will have an unusual texture.

Lay a string on a piece of paper in any arrangement you wish. Cover the string and paper with another piece of paper and rub with crayon. A line will appear with an attractive design. Do the same thing with leaves.

Place an object on a piece of manila drawing paper. Dip a toothbrush into watercolor or ink. The color is spattered by rubbing the thumb nail against the brush. The design will be determined by the amount of spattering. Remove the object from the paper when finished and a nice design will appear.

Plan a design using crepe paper or tissue paper cut in interesting shapes. Wet a large piece of white paper and place the shapes on it. Press. Lift off the shapes and a design will appear.

Draw with chalk on wet paper.

Place paper on a rough surface. Rub chalk over it for an interesting design. Experiment with different media and different surfaces.

Draw one design or place one object on a piece of paper. Have the child draw a design or picture around it.

Cut out different shapes of construction paper. Arrange them on another sheet of paper until they make an interesting design. Paste them down.

Make mosaics out of stones, weeds, beans, corn, rice, etc. Use combinations of them for interesting designs.

Cut slits in construction paper and make interesting designs by weaving strips of paper throughout the paper.

Paint some parts of a paper with rubber cement and allow to dry. Cover the paper with watercolor. After the paint dries, erase the rubber cement until white spots appear.

Paint on paper and sprinkle with various colors of glitter.

Paint with a toothbrush, feather, comb or any other device that will make an interesting design.

Center: **Science**

Purpose: To supplement and enrich formal science teaching and to gain practice in the manipulation of science materials and equipment.

Materials:

collection of objects to use in classification
magnifying glasses
microscopes
machines—motors
materials to build simple machines
gears
magnets
batteries and materials for electricity experiments
foods such as salt, flour, sugar, etc.
metric materials
animals and plants: living and pictures
materials for gardening
litmus paper
glassware
materials for making weather station
kits, tapes, filmstrips and books of all kinds
rocks, soils, collections of all kinds
musical instruments (materials to make instruments)
models of human body, simple plants, and animals
aquariums, terrariums, and incubators
candles
mirrors
iron filings
materials to show expansion and contraction
heat source
lenses, prisms, etc.
hand tools
fabrics
solutions to test with

Activities:

Put a few drops of food coloring in a beaker of water. Watch the diffusion and explain what happens.

Put 50 ml of water in a graduate. Put 50 ml of alcohol in another graduate. Add the two together. How many milliliters did you get? Why?

Build a model of various atoms.

Do a research project on nuclear energy.

Make an electromagnet.

Make a station in your center for an Elementary Science Study Kit from McGraw-Hill or a similar commercial kit.

Make parallel and series circuits. Explain the uses of these circuits.

Experiment with magnetic fields, iron filings, and magnets.

Make a telegraph set.

Run a comb through dry hair and place it near a small piece of paper. What happens? Why?

Make and demonstrate examples of the six simple machines.

Make a station in the center on the metric system.

Put a piece of steel wool in a test tube and invert it in water. Wait one day and check. What happens? Why?

Blow on a cold beaker. What happens? Why?

Punch holes in two paper cups. With the bottoms facing each other pass a long string through both holes and tie a knot in each end. By stretching the string one cup can be used as a telephone sender and the other end as a receiver. Explain what happens.

Fill a glass to the brim with water and place a small piece of cardboard over it. Invert the glass and carefully remove your hand. What happens? Why?

Invert an empty beaker over a lighted candle. What happens? Why?

Make a pinhole camera.

Make a homemade microscope.

Make a hay infusion of pond water and let it set for a week. Look at the various microorganisms with your homemade microscope.

Make a volcano.

Find as many samples of rocks as you can. Classify them.

Plant seeds. Experiment with various amounts of water, sunlight, and soil.

Put a piece of celery in a glass of colored water. What happens? Why?

Make collections of rocks, leaves, insects, bird eggs, etc.

Make a photography station in the center.

Grow crystals in the center.

Make fossils out of plaster of Paris.

Make a station in the center on pollution.

Obtain models of the human body. Study functions, parts, and diseases.

Make charts of varoius kinds of foods, minimum daily requirements, etc.

Make reports on great scientists.

Make a reed on the end of a large straw. Blow on the reed until a sound comes out. Continue to blow and at the same time cut small pieces off the end of the straw. What happens to the sound? Why?

Make a station on the harmful effects of drugs, alcohol, and tobacco.

Build a station around flight.

Set up a station showing conduction, convection and radiation.

Set up a station on various kinds of engines.

Make a station on astronomy. Make models of the solar system, galaxies, etc.

Make a sundial.

Make a station on migration, hibernation, or estivation.

Make a station on the cell.

Classify plants and animals.

Make up some job cards on oceanography.

Have many living plants and animals in your center.

Put a few drops of water in a gallon can. Heat the water until steam comes out. Quickly place the cap on the hole and place in cold water. What happens? Why?

Make a weather station.

Make a water thermometer.

Make a compass.

Classification:
    A. Select objects and classify by size, shape, color and texture.
    B. Try to classify objects while blindfolded.
    C. Cut pictures out of magazines. Classify them according to where the items might be purchased.
    D. Classify objects into edible and non-edible.
    E. Classify objects according to the states of matter.
    F. Classify objects according to sharpness and dullness.
    G. Classify objects according to absorbency and non-absorbency.
    H. Classify objects according to magnetic attraction.

Study the fossil fuels.

Make an electric motor.

Study heredity by raising fruit flies.

Center: **Music**

Purpose: To manipulate and practice with various musical instruments and
to enrich formal music teaching.

Materials:

bells	charts
rhythm instruments	listening station
various sizes of jars	autoharp
castanets	paper for writing music
chime bars	music scores
materials for making instruments	chalkboard and music staff
tambourines	piano
junk	cymbals
tuning forks	ukulele
records and tapes	glockenspiel
drums	Indian bells
records	unusual instruments
books	recorders

Activities:

Place familiar songs on charts and display in center.

Tape popular songs for listening.

Listen to records of classical music.

Tape music class or music programs in the school for the center.

Have children do reports on famous composers.

Have materials available for children to compose songs.

Play commercial games like Conn Quiz.

Make drums from hatboxes or tin cans using inner tubes as the drumhead.

Make rhythm instruments.

Practice the ukelele in the center.

Ask the children to tape solos and place them in the center for others to
listen to.

Make a set of cards for various dances that the children can learn on their
own.

Practice tinkling.

Clap out rhythms from tapes and records.

Encourage the children to form their own bands and practice during center time.

Have job cards that give the child practice in reading notes.

Have flannelboard cutouts to help children learn note reading.

Encourage the children to sharpen their storytelling skills by including music in their presentation.

Have music tests in the center.

Order films for the center.

Have a stockpile of music from other countries. When a country is studied the children can go to the music center to learn about its music.

Show video tapes of great musical performances.

Have a chart which gives the process for one child to teach a song to another.

Obtain a number of charts of the most frequently used instruments. Learn all you can about them.

Obtain records or tapes on movement. Use this to develop body awareness.

Make a set of job cards to learn musical terms.

Encourage children to bring favorite records for the center.

Center: **Manipulative Materials**

Purpose: To assure each child that he will not leave the manipulative stage of learning until such time that a sound foundation is laid for the abstract. To learn through play.

Materials:

puppets	sandbox
puppet theatre	water play materials
Lincoln logs	toys
puzzles	pick-up sticks
Tinker Toys	measuring devices
scraps of all kinds	small cars and trucks
buttons, snaps, washers, bolts, etc.	traffic signs
	clay
numeral letters: plastic, magnetic, wooden	materials for sewing
	materials for cooking
Erector sets	materials for knitting, embroidery, etc.
commercial manipulative games	
pegboards	material for cutting and pasting

wood and plastic shapes   materials for woodworking
blocks

FOOTNOTES

[1]Richard Hanson, "An Introduction to Learning Centers," *Insights* (Grand Forks, North Dakota: University of North Dakota, March, 1971). p. 2.

chapter seven

Learning to Read:
The Primary Skills Program

Reading to Learn:
The Intermediate Skills Program

The success of the child in learning to read depends primarily upon how effectively he learns the essential reading skills presented in the primary years. For this reason, particular attention must be given to reading instruction during these years. If the child learns to read well during this time, he will encounter little if any difficulty in the succeeding years. If he fails to learn to read in the primary years, however, it is most likely that he will have academic difficulties throughout his school career.

The basic foundation upon which a child's reading ability is built depends to a large extent upon his readiness to learn. If the child is not ready for formal instruction it would be wise for him to remain out of school another year, attend one of many preschool programs now available, or repeat kindergarten. It is better that the child enter Primary I when formal reading instruction begins, ready to learn, rather than meeting failure in the formal reading situation and have to repeat. In those instances where the child does enter Primary I before he is ready, the teacher should keep him in a readiness program, and then in the next year carry him on into the Primary I reading program. Depending upon a great many other circumstances, of course, it is often wise to have him repeat at this time. Retention at levels above primary is both ineffective and may actually result in even lower achievement levels than before retention.

Learning to Read: The Primary Skills Program

Because reading skills in the primary are so vitally important to the child's ability to read effectively at higher levels, the teacher must move slowly. She must be certain that each child is mastering those skills which are essential to more advanced reading. There must be a logical, sequential development of skills. Only if these skills are presented when the child is ready for them, in a manner which does not skip over certain skills, can he be expected to build an effective foundation for reading skills.

It must be recognized that learning reading skills is not the final goal, however. The teaching of skills is intended to help children read better. If skill instruction is isolated from reading itself, it is likely that all the children will not be able to make the needed connection between the two. It is not unusual to find children who are able to do some of these reading skills well but who do not know how to read. When skill instruction is not an integral part of the reading process, it is little more than another subject added to the curriculum which has little carryover either to reading or spelling. The goal of reading instruction is, of course, to help children know how to read well and to enjoy reading. To the extent that they read on their own, either to obtain information or for pleasure, the instruction is successful. How well the child has mastered reading skills is only an indication of his reading ability, and is definitely not the sole criterion by which reading ability should be measured.

It is not enough even to insist that skill instruction should be a part of reading instruction. Reading instruction itself must be a part of a still bigger picture. The language arts area, which includes reading, writing, spelling, and listening, must be considered as a total unit. Reading is only one part of this language arts area and must be kept in proper perspective.

The fragmentation of the language arts program into a large number of isolated subjects will result in less effective teaching and an actual waste of badly needed time. With pressure upon schools becoming greater and greater to teach more and more subjects, the classroom teacher cannot afford the time to break each subject down into many unrelated parts. It is necessary that she teach children to relate those things which they learn in one subject into useful learning experiences for mastering other subjects.

As isolated subjects, spelling, writing, and reading are each so much an entity unto themselves that the child cannot hope to remember all of the things that are to be learned. Phonic instruction, for example, should obviously be helpful both to reading and spelling. As spelling is practiced, there is no reason why writing should not also be practiced. The total language arts approach is not only sensible, it is absolutely necessary if the classroom teacher is to be successful either in a personalized reading program or in the basal reading program.

There is some disagreement among educational authorities as to whether or not reading skills should be presented to all children. Certain children at each level already know how to read material at that level. Whether or not these children should be taught the skills at that level is a controversy among reading specialists which will perhaps never be resolved. One solution would be to present all of the reading skills to all of the children, regardless of their actual reading level so long as it is at least at their age level, with the idea that even though the student may not need these skills at this particular point, he will need them later. The authors believe that the reason why so many bright children are such poor spellers is that they have missed the skill instruction in phonics at the primary level because they did not need it at that level to read or spell. But when they reached a higher level, they needed the phonic skill but did not have it and therefore encountered spelling problems. It is certainly true that brighter children will not spend so much time as average and slower learning children on the reading skills. It is important, however, that the skills be presented to the pupils if their achievement level is at least at grade level. If it is found that the student already knows the particular skill, then no time need be spent drilling on it. If the child does not know the particular skill, however, some time should be spent actually practicing the skill to be sure that it is mastered. The slower children will undoubtedly need more of this rote drill, but the initial presentation should be made to all the children.

Perhaps the major criticism of the personalized reading program has been that it does not pay careful attention to the teaching of reading skills. Whether or not the teacher actually follows the manual in the basal reading program, the teacher is guided through a pattern of skill presentation. The fact that many teachers do not use the teachers' manual, or change from one basal series in one grade to another, is a problem of application and should not be considered a weakness of the basal reading program itself. The personalized reading program does allow for more flexibility of program so that it is possible for skill instruction to be neglected. The experienced teacher, however, should know those skills which she would need to teach. The beginning teacher is not in a position to know these skills quite so well, however. But both the experienced teacher and the beginning teacher need some kind of guide to follow in a more condensed form than the teachers' manual, whether they are teaching in the personalized program or in the basal reader. It is for this reason that the skills check lists that follow were developed.

We believe that the most important skills to be developed are the readiness skills. If the child is adequately *prepared* for formal skill instruction, he will encounter success in it. Initial success in the learning-to-read process must be recognized as a major factor in good reading. Initial failure in the learning-to-read process is probably the major cause of subsequent failure in all academic areas.

After the readiness skills check list all others are arranged by grade level. By arranging these skills at grade level, we do not mean that all children in each grade should be reading at this level. The teacher should be concerned with the skills mastered by each particular child, and should work accordingly with him. His actual grade placement may be little more than an indication of his chronological age. It is an impractical teacher indeed who insists that because she has a Primary III class she is going to insist upon every child reading at Primary III level. Such a situation would indeed be ideal, but in practice it does not exist.

The skills listed at each level are those which must be mastered at that level. Once they have been learned, the child is ready to move to the next level. As indicated in Chapter 5, copies of these skills check list should be kept in each child's folder so it is possible for the teacher to determine exactly those skills which have been learned and those which need more reinforcement. In some cases it will be necessary to review or actually reteach certain of the skills, but by noting whether or not the skill has been checked, it is possible for the teacher to determine if this skill is a new one for the child or one merely to be relearned.

At the beginning of each year after the child has completed his first year in school, the teacher would be wise to review briefly those skills which were presented and learned at the preceding level. This might be the first type of group which is established. As the skills are reviewed, the teacher will quickly come to know those children who have thoroughly retained those skills which they have learned, as well as those who will need more review work in the skills of the earlier level. Remembering that the purpose of establishing groups in the personalized program is to accomplish a particular goal, these groups will be disbanded as soon as the review skills have been covered.

Reading to Learn: The Intermediate Skills Program

Insofar as intermediate reading skills are concerned, they have often been overlooked as a subject which needs to be taught at the upper elementary levels. Even though the basal reader has attempted to provide teachers with a teachers' manual, too frequently the upper elementary teacher has been so overburdened with the wide variety of subjects to be taught that reading has suffered. In too many situations, reading has not actually been taught as a skill subject. The grades in reading which were put on the report card were only a reflection on how well the child was able to read when he arrived at the intermediate level. It in no way indicated the progress which he had made in reading. This was not a fault of the basal reader approach, but is a problem which must be faced regardless of the type of reading program.

Reading skills which are introduced at the intermediate level are, to a large part, a review and refinement of skills already presented at the primary levels. But because of a variety of factors, not least among these is the lack of readiness on the part of many of the children for the skills which were presented earlier, some children arrive at the intermediate levels not knowing primary level skills. There are new reading skills to be presented at the intermediate level also. If a child can only learn primary skills or upper intermediate level skills, he certainly should know the primary skills first. But learning reading skills should not be an either-or proposition, but rather should be a continuous development of sequential skills designed to provide the child with the highest possible degree of independence in reading. Merely the development of a higher reading level score because of an ever-increasing reading vocabulary does not promote the maximum amount of reading improvement.

A formal reading period should continue throughout the elementary years. The personalized reading program, which allows children to select the material which they wish to read, can most easily be worked into the reading required in the content subjects. For those teachers doing unit teaching, the personalized reading program offers the opportunity for the child to do independent reading to meet special needs in content areas.

Dangers in Intermediate Skill Instruction

The beginning of the intermediate years is distinctive in American public education in that emphasis moves away from instruction for the purpose of learning skills to use of this skill to learn content material. This transition is fraught with dangers. Among the more important ones are:

1. It is too often assumed that all children have mastered basic reading skills of the primary levels so that these skills are not reviewed or retaught.

2. The overcrowded schedule, in which the teacher is expected to cover a great number of different subjects, results in reading being left out of the formal teaching curriculum.

3. Some children, particularly those with better than average abilities, have relied upon their superior memories to learn new words. With the introduction of content subjects, the student is unable to remember all of the new words, and sometimes develops a dislike for what seems to him to be a new type of reading.

4. Fewer intermediate teachers than primary teachers know the "what" and "how" of teaching reading.

5. The shifting away of the great desire within each child to please his parents and the teacher, into a stronger desire to gain the approval of his peer group, means that the attitude of the child's peer group toward reading must be good. If the children do not like reading, there is a growing attitude at this age which will increasingly influence adversely the attitude of other children toward reading.

The review of the primary reading skills comes as well as the introduction of new skills at the intermediate levels. The personalized reading program offers the teacher the best opportunity for going back to the level at which each child needs instruction, and moving him as rapidly as possible to higher levels of skill development.

BARBE READING SKILLS CHECK LIST
READINESS LEVEL

_____ (Last Name)

_____ (First Name)

_____ (Name of School)

_____ (Name of Teacher)

_____ (Age)

_____ (Grade Placement)

I. Vocabulary:

A. Word Recognition

____ 1. Interested in words and symbols

____ 2. Recognizes own name in print

____ 3. Names upper-case letters

____ 4. Names lower-case letters

____ 5. Matches upper-case and lower-case letters

____ 6. Identifies numerals 1-10

B. Word Meaning

____ 1. Listening vocabulary adequate to understand ideas

____ 2. Speaking vocabulary adequate to convey ideas

3. Comprehends meaning of:

Place words	Quantitative words	Descriptive words
____ here	____ number words 1-10	____ color words
____ under	____ many	____ size words
____ in	____ more	____ shape words
____ near	____ much	____ same
____ up	____ some	____ different
____ right	____ all	____ alike
____ there		
____ over		
____ out		
____ far		
____ down		
____ left		

____ 4. Recognizes spoken words with same initial sound

____ 5. Recognizes spoken words with same final sound

____ 6. Hears rhyming words

B. Visual

1. Sees likenesses and differences in:

____ colors

____ shapes and designs

____ directionality and size

____ letters

____ words

____ 2. Recognizes word boundaries

____ 3. Visualizes part-to-whole by assembling 7-piece puzzle

____ 4. Left to right eye movement

III. Comprehension

A. Interest

____ 1. Wants to learn to read

____ 2. Enjoys being read to

____ 3. Shows interest in books and other printed materials

front _____ back _____ none
top _____ bottom _____ most
beside _____ next to _____ few
above _____ below _____ whole
inside _____ outside _____ part
middle _____ between _____ half
beginning _____ end
on _____ through
first _____ last
second _____ third
around _____ behind
before

4. Classifies objects and pictures into logical categories
5. Aware that printed words represent spoken words

II. Perceptive Skills

A. Auditory

1. Reproduces pronounced two and three syllable words
2. Hears minimal differences in words (Are these the same or different? hat-hit, pot-cot, cat-cap)
3. Able to hear word length (Which is the shorter word? boy-elephant)

B. Ability

1. Adequate attention span
2. Remembers from stories read aloud:
    main ideas
    names of characters
    some major details
3. Can sequence events logically
4. Follows oral directions
5. Looks at books:
    from front to back
    from left-hand page to right-hand page
6. Aware of usual text progression:
    from left to right
    from top to bottom

IV. Oral Expression

A. Expresses self spontaneously

B. Expresses complete thoughts (sentences)

C. Able to remember and reproduce a five-word sentence

D. Can retell a story in his own words

Teacher's Notes

155

BARBE READING SKILLS CHECK LIST
FIRST LEVEL

_____ (Last Name)   _____ (First Name)   _____ (Name of School)

_____ (Age)   _____ (Grade Placement)   _____ (Name of Teacher)

I. Vocabulary:
A. Word Recognition
1. Recognizes words with both upper and lower-case letters at beginning
2. Knows names of letters in sequence
3. Is able to identify in various settings the following words usually found in preprimers and primers:

__ a	__ eat	__ look	__ TV
__ about	__ farm	__ make	__ table
__ again	__ father	__ man	__ take
__ all	__ fast	__ many	__ thank
__ am	__ find	__ may	__ that
__ an	__ fine	__ me	__ the
__ and	__ fish	__ mitten	__ their
__ apple	__ for	__ mother	__ them
__ are	__ from	__ more	__ then
__ as	__ fun	__ morning	__ there
__ at	__ funny	__ must	__ they
__ away	__ get	__ my	__ this
__ baby	__ girl	__ near	__ tree
__ back	__ give	__ new	__ to
__ ball	__ go	__ night	__ too
__ be	__ good	__ no	__ toy
__ bed	__ good-by	__ not	__ two
__ been	__ green	__ of	__ up
__ big	__ has	__ on	__ us
__ birthday	__ had	__ one	__ walk
__ black	__ happy	__ or	__ want

3. Discriminates between words using:
   initial letter cues
   (Which word is hat? hat-foot) ___
   final letter cues
   (Which word is bear? bear-boat) ___
4. Associates sounds to digraphs:
   sh ___   th (this and thin) ___
   wh ___   ch (church) ___
5. Associates sounds to two letter blends:

st ___	fr ___	gr ___	sw ___
bl ___	fl ___	sp ___	br ___
pl ___	cl ___	sm ___	gr ___
tr ___	gl ___	sn ___	sl ___

6. Knows that the letters a, e, i, o, u, and combinations of these can represent several different sounds

B. Structural Analysis
1. Knows endings
   ed sound as "ed" in wanted
   ed sound as "d" in moved
   ed sound as "t" in liked
2. Recognizes compound words
   (into, upon)
3. Knows common word families

all ___	an ___	ell ___	ook ___	in ___
at ___	ill ___	ay ___	ing ___	ish ___
it ___	et ___	ake ___	ack ___	ight ___

C. Word Form Clues
1. Recognizes upper and lower-case letters

156

blue	have	party	was
boat	he	pie	water
boy	help	play	way
but	her	pretty	we
by	here	puppy	went
cake	hide	put	were
call	him	rabbit	what
came	his	ran	when
can	home	red	where
car	house	ride	which
Christmas	how	run	white
come	I	said	who
cookies	if	sat	will
could	in	saw	wish
cow	is	see	with
cowboy	it	she	woman
daddy	jump	show	work
day	just	sleep	would
did	kitten	so	yellow
dinner	know	some	yes
dish	laugh	something	you
do	let	soon	your
dog	like	splash	
down	little	stop	
	long	surprise	

II. Word Analysis:

A. Sound-symbol Associations

1. Associates consonant sounds to the following letters:

b ___	h ___	n ___	t ___
c (cat) ___	j ___	p ___	v ___
d ___	k ___	q ___	w ___
f ___	l ___	r ___	y ___
g (goat) ___	m ___	s ___	z ___

2. Names letters to represent consonant sounds heard in:

initial position

final position

medial position

III. Comprehension

A. Understands that printed symbols represent objects or actions

B. Can follow printed directions

C. Can draw conclusions from given facts

D. Can recall from stories read aloud:
- main idea
- names of characters
- important details
- stated sequence

E. Can recall after silent reading:
- main idea
- names of characters
- important details
- stated sequence

F. Can distinguish between real and imaginary events

G. Uses context clues in word attack

H. Can suggest or select an appropriate title for a story

I. Can relate story content to own experiences

IV. Oral and Silent Reading Skills:

A. Oral Reading

1. Uses correct pronunciation

2. Uses correct phrasing (not word-by-word)

3. Uses proper voice intonation to give meaning

4. Has good posture and handles book appropriately

5. Understands simple punctuation:
- period (.)
- comma (,)
- question mark (?)
- exclamation mark (!)

B. Silent Reading

1. Reads without vocalization:
- Lip movements
- Whispering

2. Reads without head movements

BARBE READING SKILLS CHECK LIST
SECOND LEVEL

_____ (Last Name) _____ (First Name) _____ (Name of School)

_____ (Age) _____ (Grade Placement) _____ (Name of Teacher)

I. Vocabulary:

A. Word Recognition

1. Recognizes 220 Dolch Basic Sight Words (by end of year)

a	as	again	about	any
all	away	ate	after	better
am	be	but	always	both
an	black	cold	around	bring
and	brown	cut	ask	carry
are	by	fast	because	clean
at	came	first	been	could
big	did	five	before	done
blue	eat	fly	best	don't
call	fall	four	buy	draw
can	find	give	does	drink
come	for	goes	far	eight
do	from	going	found	every
down	get	got	full	hurt
funny	have	green	gave	know
go	her	had	grow	light
good	him	has	hold	myself
he	his	hot	how	never
help	if	its	just	own
here	into	long	keep	pick
I	laugh	made	kind	right
in	let	many	much	seven
is	live	new	must	shall
it	may	not	now	show
jump	my	of	off	their
like	no	open	once	them
little	old	or	only	then

oo as in book —
oo as in balloon —
ike as in like —
eck as in neck —

aw as in straw —
ew as in new —
ock as in clock —
ack as in back —

ind as in find —
ing as in sing —

6. Short vowel sounds (a, o, i, u, e)
7. Long vowel sounds
8. Understands function of "y" as a consonant at beginning of word (yard) and vowel (bicycle) anywhere else
9. Knows two sounds of c and g:
   C followed by i, e or y makes s sound
   C followed by a, o or u makes k sound (examples: city, cent and cat, cot)
   G followed by i, e or y makes j sound
   G followed by a, o or u makes guh sound (examples: ginger, gym and game, gun)
10. Knows initial consonant sound includes all consonants up to first vowel
11. Phonics rules:
    a. A single vowel in a word or syllable is usually short (hat)
    b. A single e at the end of a word makes the preceding vowel long (hate)
    c. Final y makes the sound of long i or e
    d. When there are two vowels together, the first is long and the second silent (pail, train)
    e. Vowels are influenced when followed by "r," "w," and "l"
       star
       saw
       all

look __	on __	our __	round __	there __
make __	one __	please __	sleep __	these __
me __	put __	pull __	small __	think __
out __	said __	read __	take __	those __
play __	see __	saw __	tell __	together __
pretty __	she __	say __	thank __	use __
ran __	sit __	sing __	that __	very __
red __	some __	six __	they __	want __
ride __	stop __	soon __	this __	warm __
run __	three __	start __	too __	wash __
see __	today __	ten __	try __	went __
so __	two __	upon __	under __	what __
the __	was __	us __	walk __	when __
to __	will __	who __	well __	where __
up __	work __	why __	were __	which __
we __	yes __	wish __	white __	would __
you __	yellow __	your __	with __	write __

2. Use word form clues
   a. Configuration
   b. Visual similarity of rhyming words (call, fall, ball) __

B. Word Meaning
1. Multiple meanings of words
2. Synonymous meanings (jolly-happy)
3. Opposites (up—down)
4. Words pronounced the same (rode—road)

II. Word Analysis:
A. Phonics
1. Knows consonant sounds (b, d, f, h, j, k, l, m, n, p, q, r, s, t, v, w, x, y, z)
2. Applies these sounds to:
   a. initial position in words (let)
   b. final position in words (bank)
   c. medial position in words (little)
3. Knows blends (br, cr, dr, fr, gr, pr, ur, st, sm, sn, sw, bl, cl, fl, gl, pl, sh, ch, wh, th)
4. Knows three letter initial blends:

| str __ | thr __ | spl __ |
| sch __ | spr __ | chr __ |

5. Knows word families:

ou as in *out* __	er as in *her* __	oi as in *oil* __
ow as in *show* __	ur as in *fur* __	oy as in *boy* __
ow as in *cow* __	ir as in *bird* __	ight as in *night* __

B. Structural Analysis
1. Recognizes little words in big words (*many*)
2. Recognizes compound words (*barnyard*)
3. Understands use of possessive (*Mary's*)
4. Knows contractions:

I'm __	we're __	it's __	isn't __	don't __
I've __	you're __	let's __	we've __	won't __
I'll __	they're __	she's __	he's __	can't __

5. Recognizes root words
6. Use of accented syllable introduced
7. Can alphabetize words using first and second letter

III. Comprehension:
A. Association of ideas of material read
1. Can draw conclusions
2. Can predict outcomes
3. Can find proof
4. Can associate text with pictures
B. Organization of ideas
1. Can follow printed directions
2. Can find main idea
3. Can follow plot sequence
C. Locating information
1. Can use:
   table of contents
   page number
   titles
2. Can find specific information
D. Appreciation
1. Able to dramatize stories read
2. Able to illustrate stories read
3. Able to tell a story which has been read previously
4. Owns at least several books which he particularly likes

IV. Oral and Silent Reading:
A. Oral Reading
1. Reads clearly and distinctly
2. Reads with expression
3. Reads without reversals
B. Silent Reading
1. Reads without lip or head movements
2. Reads more rapidly silently than orally

BARBE READING SKILLS CHECK LIST
THIRD LEVEL

_____ (Last Name)   _____ (First Name)   _____ (Name of School)

_____ (Age)   _____ (Grade Placement)   _____ (Name of Teacher)

I. Vocabulary:

Recognizes Dolch 220 Basic Sight Words

a	done	if	out	these
about	don't	in	over	they
after	down	into	own	think
again	draw	is	pick	this
all	drink	it	play	those
always	eat	its	please	three
am	eight	jump	pretty	to
an	every	just	pull	today
and	fall	keep	put	together
any	far	kind	ran	too
are	fast	know	read	try
around	find	laugh	red	two
as	first	let	ride	under
ask	five	light	right	up
at	fly	like	round	upon
ate	for	little	run	us
away	found	live	said	use
be	four	long	saw	very
because	from	look	say	walk
been	full	made	see	want
before	funny	make	seven	warm
best	gave	many	shall	was
better	get	may	she	wash
big	give	me	show	we
black	go	much	sing	well
blue	goes	must	sit	went
both	going	my	six	were
bring	good		sleep	what

II. Word Analysis:

A. Refine phonics skills:

1. All initial consonant sounds
2. Short and long vowel sounds
3. Changes in words by:
   a. adding s, es, d, ed, ing, er, est
   b. dropping final e and adding ing
   c. doubling the consonant before adding ing
   d. changing y to i before adding es
4. Vowel rules
   a. vowel in one syllable word is short
   b. vowel in syllable or word ending in e is long
   c. two vowels together, first is often long and second is silent
   d. vowel alone in word is short
5. C followed by i, e, y makes s sound
   C followed by a, o, u makes k sound
6. G followed by i, e, y makes j sound
   G followed by a, o, u makes guh sound
7. Silent letters in kn, wr, gn

B. Knows skills of:

1. Forming plurals
   by adding s, es, ies
   by changing f to v and adding es
2. Similarities of sound such as x and cks (box—blocks)
3. Can read Roman numerals I, V, X

C. Syllabication rules

1. There are usually as many syllables in a word as there are vowels

160

2. Where there is a single consonant between two vowels, the vowel goes with the first syllable (pu/pil)
3. When there is a double consonant, the syllable break is between the two consonants and one is silent (example: lit/tle)
D. Can hyphenate words using syllable rules
E. Understands use of primary accent mark
F. Knows to accent first syllable, unless it is a prefix, otherwise accent second syllable

III. Comprehension:
A. Can find main idea in story
B. Can keep events in proper sequence
C. Can draw logical conclusions
D. Is able to see relationships
E. Can predict outcomes
F. Can follow printed directions
G. Can read for a definite purpose:
  1. for pleasure
  2. to obtain answer to question
  3. to obtain general idea of content
H. Classify items
I. Use index
J. Alphabetize words by first two letters
K. Knows technique of skimming
L. Can determine what source to obtain information (dictionary, encyclopedia, index, glossary, etc.)
M. Use maps and charts

IV. Oral and Silent Reading:
A. Oral Reading
  1. Reads with expression
  2. Comprehends material read aloud
B. Silent Reading
  1. Reads silently without finger pointing, lip movements
  2. Comprehends material read silently
  3. Reads faster silently than orally
C. Listening
  1. Comprehends material read aloud by another
  2. Can follow directions read aloud

brown	got	myself	small	when
but	green	never	so	where
buy	grow	new	some	which
by	had	no	soon	white
call	has	not	start	who
came	have	now	stop	why
can	he	of	take	will
carry	help	off	tell	wish
clean	her	old	ten	with
cold	here	on	thank	work
come	him	once	that	would
could	his	one	the	write
cut	hot	only	their	yes
did	how	open	them	yellow
do	hurt	or	then	you
does		our	there	your

B. Word Meaning
1. Comprehends and uses correctly the following words:

Function Words
—against
—also
—being
—during
—each
—end
—enough
—men
—more
—most
—other
—same
—should
—since
—such
—than
—though
—thought
—through
—while
—women

Direction Words
—around
—backward
—forward
—left
—right
—toward

Action Words
—carry
—draw
—kick
—push
—skate
—swim
—think
—throw
—travel

Form of Address
—Miss
—Mr.
—Mrs.
—Ms.

Career Words
—artist
—factory
—lawyer
—mechanic
—money
—nurse
—office
—operator
—teacher
—training
—vacation

Color Words
—brown
—green
—orange
—purple

Metric Words
—centigrade
—gram
—liter
—meter

Curriculum Words
—add
—American
—country
—ecology
—even
—fall
—few
—greater
—less
—number
—odd
—seasons
—set
—space
—spring
—state
—subtract
—summer
—United States
—winter
—world

BARBE READING SKILLS CHECK LIST
FOURTH LEVEL

_____ (Last Name) _____ (First Name) _____ (Name of School)

_____ (Age) _____ (Grade Placement) _____ (Name of Teacher)

I. Vocabulary:

A. Word Recognition

1. Knows new words in content fields _____
2. Recognizes similarities of known words
   a. compound words _____
   b. root words _____
   c. suffixes, prefixes _____
   d. plurals _____
   e. hyphenated words _____
   f. contractions _____
3. Recognizes unusual characteristics of words _____

B. Word Meaning

1. Develops ability in getting meaning from context _____
2. Uses new words in sentences to show meaning _____
3. Knows punctuation
   a. italics _____
   b. quotation marks _____
   c. parenthesis _____
   d. exclamation marks _____
4. Use of map skills _____

II. Word Attack Skills:

A. Structural analysis

1. Knows and applies rules for syllables
   a. Each syllable must contain a vowel and a single vowel can be a syllable _____
   b. Suffixes and prefixes are syllables with meanings of their own _____
   c. The root word is not divided _____
   d. If the first vowel is followed by two consonants, the first syllable usually ends with the first consonant (example: pen cil) _____
   e. If the first vowel is followed by a single consonant, the consonant usually begins the second syllable (example: a maze, am ple) _____
   f. If a word ends in le preceded by a consonant, that consonant begins the last syllable _____
   g. The letter x always goes with the preceding vowel to form a syllable (example: ex it) _____

post _____ (after) postscript _____
ab _____ (from) abnormal _____
trans _____ (across) translate _____
em _____ (in) embark _____
de _____ (from) depart _____
inter _____ (between) interurban _____
pro _____ (in front of) promote _____
ex _____ (out of or out) explain _____
en _____ (in) enter _____
ob _____ (against) object _____
per _____ (fully, through) perfect _____

B. Phonic analysis

1. Knows phonic skills
   a. Single consonants and blends _____
   b. Short and long vowels _____
   c. Vowel teams:
      ee _____ au _____ oi _____
      ea _____ aw _____ oy _____
      ai _____ oa _____ ou _____
      ay _____ oo _____ ow _____
2. Knows vowel rules
   a. In attacking a vowel sound try first the short sound; if the word then doesn't make sense try the long sound. _____
   b. Vowels are usually short when they appear as single vowels and are followed by a consonant. _____
   c. Vowels are usually given the long sound when they appear alone and are the last letters of a word. _____
   d. When two vowels appear together in a word, the first vowel is long and the second is silent. _____
   e. In short word containing two vowels where one of the vowels is a final e, the first vowel will have a long sound while the final e is silent. _____

162

h. The letters ck go with the preceding vowel and end the syllable (example: chick en)

2. Knows accent clues
   a. The first syllable is usually accented, unless it is a prefix
   b. Beginning syllables de, re, be, in and a are usually unaccented
   c. Endings that form syllables are usually unaccented (run ning)
   d. ck following a single vowel is accented (example: jack et)

3. Knows suffixes and prefixes:
   a. Suffixes:

ness	(being)	sickness
ment	(result of)	movement
ward	(in direction of)	backward
ous	(full of)	joyous
ious	(abounding in)	gracious
et	(little)	leaflet
able	(capable of being)	capable
ic	(like, made of)	magic
ish	(like)	foolish
ant	(being)	vacant
ent	(one who)	president
age	(collection of)	baggage
ance	(state of being)	disturbance
ence	(state or quality)	violence
wise	(ways)	crosswise
ling	(little)	duckling
ty	(state)	unity
ure	(denoting action)	pleasure
ion	(condition or quality)	action

   b. Prefixes:

dis	(not, apart)	dismiss
in	(not)	invade
mis	(wrong)	mistake
anti	(against)	anticlimax
non	(not)	nonsense
com	(with)	combine
con	(with)	connect
pre	(before)	prepare
super	(over)	superior
tri	(three)	tricycle
sub	(under)	submarine

C. Uses dictionary and glossary
   1. Alphabetical Order:
      a. Order of letters in alphabet
      b. Alphabetical arrangement of words
   2. Knows to divide the dictionary to determine in which 1/3 or 1/4 the word may be found
   3. Knows the meaning and use of the phonetic spelling that follows in parenthesis each word in the dictionary
   4. Knows the use of the pronunciation key
   5. Knows to select the meaning which fits best according to the context in which the word is used
   6. Knows the meaning and use of guide words
   7. Knows the meaning and use of the secondary accent mark

III. Comprehension:
A. Finding the main idea
   1. Choosing title for material read
   2. Can identify key words and topic sentences
   3. Summarizing
B. Finding details
   1. Finding specific information
   2. Interpreting descriptive words and phrases
   3. Selecting facts to remember
   4. Selecting facts to support main idea
   5. Using study guides, charts, outlines
   6. Verifying answers
   7. Arranging ideas in sequence
C. Creative reading
   1. Able to interpret story ideas (generalize)
   2. Able to see relationships
   3. Able to identify the mood of a reading selection
   4. Able to identify author's purpose
   5. Able to identify character traits
D. Formal outlining
   1. Form
      a. Main ideas (I, II, III)
      b. Subordinate ideas (A, B, C)
   2. Talking from an outline

IV. Oral and Silent Reading:
A. Understands material at grade level
B. Eye-voice span of three words in oral reading

BARBE READING SKILLS CHECK LIST
FIFTH LEVEL

_____ _____ _____
(Last Name)   (First Name)   (Name of School)

_____ _____ _____
(Age)   (Grade Placement)   (Name of Teacher)

I. Vocabulary:

A. Word recognition of vocabulary in content areas
Social Studies—English—Arithmetic—Science—Miscellaneous

B. Meaning of words
1. Can define word read in context
2. Can provide synonyms, antonyms
3. Knows homophones (deer, dear)
4. Knows homographs (fast: run/not eat)
5. Understands figurative and colorful expressions

II. Word Attack Skills:

A. Phonics skills
1. Syllabication
   a. Each syllable must contain a vowel and a single vowel can be a syllable

6. Can follow cross-references
7. Understands secondary accent (lé vi)

C. Context clues
1. Uses context clues
2. Understands sentence structure (noun, verb)

III. Comprehension:

A. Locating information
1. Can locate: title page, author, illustrations, publisher, copyright year, and index
2. Uses table of contents

B. Note taking
1. Can take notes from reading
2. Can take notes from lecture

C. Organizing material correctly
1. Uses Roman numerals and letters in outlining
2. Can list ideas in proper sequence
3. Can follow directions
4. Can summarize

D. Uses reference materials effectively
1. The encyclopedia:
   a. Understands topics arranged alphabetically

164

b. The root or base word is a syllable and is not divided
c. Blends are not divided (bl/str)
d. Suffixes and prefixes are syllables (dust y   in come)
e. If the vowel in a syllable is followed by two consonants, the syllable usually ends with the first consonant (dif fer)
f. If a vowel in a syllable is followed by only one consonant, the syllable usually ends with a vowel (pu pil)
g. If a word ends in le, the consonant just before the l begins the last syllable (peo ple)
h. When there is an r after a vowel, the r goes with the vowel (ar gue)

2. Vowel sounds (review long and short sounds)
a. With only one vowel in a word or syllable, the vowel is short
b. With two vowels in a word or syllable, the first vowel is long and the second is silent

3. Accent
a. In a word of 2 or more syllables, the first syllable is usually accented unless it is a prefix.
b. Accent is usually on root of word

B. Using a dictionary
1. Alphabetization:
a. Division into quarters: a-f; g-m; n-r; s-z
b. Alphabetizing word through fourth letter
c. Knows abbreviated parts of speech as n.; v.; adj.; and adv.
2. Uses guide words at top of page
3. Uses diacritical markings (bottom of page)
4. Uses key to pronunciations (bottom of page)
5. Understands phonetic spellings

b. Knows meaning of characters on back of each volume
c. Knows different uses of dictionaries and encyclopedias

2. The atlas and maps:
a. Can use local maps to check known facts about streets and highways
b. Can use atlas to find answers for questions on location, relative size, direction, and distance
c. Can use maps to explain latitude and longitude
3. Use of magazines and newspapers to supply recent information
4. Can locate occupational information

E. Can interpret graphs and charts
1. Knows meaning of line graphs
2. Knows meaning of bar graphs
3. Can read charts
F. Knows metric terms and can interpret them
G. Reading for appreciation
1. Reads for pleasure
2. Reads from variety of sources: books (fiction and non-fiction), magazines, etc.
3. Reads several things by the same author

IV. Oral and Silent Reading
A. Oral Reading
1. Reads with understanding and expression
2. Varies rate of oral reading depending on material
3. Can read without constantly looking at material
B. Silent Reading
1. Reads silently more rapidly than orally
2. Reads with good comprehension
3. Reads without lip or head movements or pointing
4. Enjoys reading silently

BARBE READING SKILLS CHECK LIST
SIXTH LEVEL

_____ (Last Name) _____ (First Name) _____ (Name of School)

_____ (Age) _____ (Grade Placement) _____ (Name of Teacher)

I. Vocabulary:

A. Word recognition
1. Uses context clues
   a. How the word is used in a sentence
   b. Function of word
2. Uses configuration clues
   a. visual impressions of words
   b. shape, length of words
3. Uses language rhythms
   a. Rhyming clues
   b. Appreciation for general rhythm of well-expressed ideas

B. Knows and uses prefixes and suffixes

Prefix	Meaning	Suffix	Meaning
ab	from, away	able, ible	capable of being
an	without, not	acy, ace, ancy,	
ad	to, toward	ance	state of being
ante	before	an, ean, ian	one who
bi	two, twice	age	act or condition
circum	around	ant	n.—one who,
de	from		relating to, like
dis	apart, not	er, ar	n.—one who—(place
dia	around	ary	where)
ex	out of, from		adj.—relating to
im	not, in		
il, un, in, ir	into, not	en	one who is little,
			made
inter	between	ence	state of quality
in, en	in, into, among	ent	adj.—being, n.—one who
intro	within, against	full	full of
mis	wrong, wrongly	fy, ify	to make
non	not	hood	state, condition
pan	whole, all	ic	like, made of
per	fully, through	ice	that which, quality or
peri	around, about		state of being
post	after, behind	id	being in a condition of

C. Syllabication
1. Knows rules for syllables
   a. Each syllable must have a vowel and a single vowel can be a syllable
   b. The root word is a syllable and not divided
   c. Blends are not divided (th, str, wh, etc.)
   d. Suffixes and prefixes are syllables
   e. Suffix—ed if preceded by a single d or t usually forms separate syllable (rest ed)
   f. If vowel in a syllable is followed by two consonants, the syllable ends with the first consonant
   g. If vowel in a syllable is followed by only one consonant, the syllable ends with a vowel
   h. If a word ends in le, the consonant just before the l begins the last syllable (ta-ble han-dle)
   i. When there is an r after a vowel, the r goes with the vowel

D. Knows accent rules
1. In a word of two or more syllables, the first syllable is usually accented unless it is a prefix
2. In most two syllable words that end in a consonant followed by y, the first syllable is accented and the last is unaccented
3. Beginning syllables de, re, be, er, in, and a are usually not accented
4. When a suffix is added, the accent falls on or within the root word
5. Endings that form syllables are usually unaccented
6. When a final syllable ends in le, that syllable is usually not accented

E. Knows possessives
F. Knows contractions
G. Knows silent letters
H. Glossary

pre — before
pro — for, in front of
re — back, again
se — aside
semi — half, partly
sub — under
super — over, above
trans — beyond, across
tri — three, thrice
un — not

ion — act or state of being
ize, ise — to make
ist, ite — one who
ity, ty — state
ive — relating to
less — without
ly — in a way
ment — act or state of being
ness — state of being
or, ar, er, ory — one who, that which
ose, ous — abounding in
some — full of
ward — turning to, in direction
y — like or full of

C. Word Meaning
1. Knows multiple meanings of words
2. Can associate words and feelings
3. Formal and informal language
   a. Identifies different speech patterns
   b. Understands level of language usage
4. Distinguishes between aided and unaided recall
5. Can hyphenate words
6. Can provide synonyms
7. Can provide antonyms
8. Understands homophones (same sound, different spelling: *some—sum*)
9. Understands homographs (same spelling, different meaning: run *fast—fast* from food)
10. Can write metaphors
11. Can write similies

II. Word Attack Skills:
A. Phonic and structural characteristics of words
1. Knows initial consonants and blends
2. Knows short and long vowels
B. Vowel sounds
1. Knows vowel rules
   a. When there is only one vowel in a word or syllable, the vowel is short
   b. When there are two vowels in a word or syllable, the first vowel is long and the second is silent
   c. When there are two vowels together, the first vowel is long and the second is silent

III. Comprehension:
A. Outlining.
1. Takes notes effectively
2. Can sequence ideas or events
3. Can skim for specific purposes:
   a. To locate facts and details
   b. To select and reject materials to fit a certain purpose
4. Can identify main ideas of paragraphs
5. Can interpret characters' feelings
6. Can identify topic sentences
B. Following directions
C. Drawing conclusions
D. Reading for verification
E. Locating information
1. Reference material:
   a. Can read and interpret graphs
   b. Can read and interpret maps
   c. Can locate materials in encyclopedia
   d. Uses dictionary regularly
2. Library skills:
   a. Uses card catalog
   b. Understands book classification system
   c. Has library card
3. Periodical reading:
   a. Reads newspapers regularly
   b. Knows major sections of newspapers
   c. Reads magazines regularly
   d. Uses periodicals for current information
F. Can read proof marks:
paragraph ¶   upper-case ≡
delete ⌇   lower-case /
insert ∧   transpose
insert period ⊙   insert comma ∧

IV. Oral and Silent Reading
A. Oral Reading
1. Reads aloud with expression
2. Reads with confidence and correct phrasing
B. Silent Reading
1. Reads without lip movements
2. Adjusts rate depending on material being read
3. Can read 180 words per minute in fiction at grade level

Summary

The teaching of reading skills is not an end in itself. Not all children will need to learn all of those skills which have been presented. The presentation of these skills, however, without requiring a great amount of repetition or drill on them should make the student better able to read. Only to the extent that the teacher incorporates these skills in the actual reading process itself will they be successful, however.

The personalized reading program offers the teacher a great opportunity to combine teaching of reading skills along with reading itself in material of the child's own selection. This should develop both better reading abilities as well as a greater appreciation for literature. To the extent that the student is able to enjoy both "the process and the results," the reading teacher truly has been successful.

chapter eight

Evaluating Personalized
Reading Instruction

Is personalized reading better than any of the other methods of teaching reading? Like every other reading evaluation study of the past, that question cannot be answered with a simple yes or no. While there is little actual research evidence to indicate that the personalized reading program is truly superior to the basal reader approach, neither is there evidence to support the belief that it is not superior. In philosophy it is certainly easy to determine that the personalized approach is sound, but the comparison of groups being taught by one method as opposed to another is always subject to some question. As has been discussed, most often research reports show the superiority of any new method. The very factor of change alone seems to make for improvement. Increased interest in a new program is always another contributing factor. Keeping these facts in mind, and remembering that the personalized program is not just one set of procedures but rather many adaptions of Olson's principles of seeking, self-selection, and pacing, we must nevertheless realize that examination of the research literature has value.

Evaluation must concern itself with many factors. A factor such as improvement in both knowledge and application of skills is indeed important and can in part be measured by determining the level of reading at the beginning of the year and at the end of the year. But there are other factors which are of equal importance. These factors may easily be forgotten in an evaluation, perhaps partially because they cannot be measured so easily. They include such intangibles as enjoyment of reading, interest in what Witty[1] has referred to as both the process and the results of reading, and the actual use of critical reading in everyday practice.

It is in these intangible areas that the personalized reading proponents claim the greatest gain. When the factors themselves cannot be carefully defined (for they relate to attitude, which is one of the hardest possible areas of human behavior to describe) statistical evaluation is very difficult. Essentially, then, it appears that the personalized program is difficult to evaluate in terms of its very strongest aspects and must depend, to a large extent, upon evaluation of those areas in which it is most like the basal reading program.

The very fact that the personalized reading program is an individual program adds to the difficulty in evaluating it. For the personalized program to be successful it must be flexible and indeed different; therefore, the statistician is likely to be dissatisfied with the evaluation reports which are appearing in the literature.

The "action research" type of study is apparently the most common type of report available. This is the description of the program in operation in one particular level or school system and a report on how the teacher or author felt that the program helped the children make progress toward better reading. It is not meant to be indicative of a so-called "typical" situation, nor even of ideal conditions. It is more or less what happened in one situation. This type of reporting is of little real value for others when taken alone, but when combined with the reports of others in different situations and other parts of the country, the reports gain in value. It is mostly upon this type of research that the personalized program must now be evaluated.

Evaluation should be made in a variety of ways. Essentially, the evaluations will probably be based on (1) test results; (2) some measure of the number of books read and the variety of types of books read; and (3) some measure of attitudes of both parents and children toward the program and toward reading itself.

Test results may be used in a variety of ways. They are undoubtedly the easiest way to evaluate the program, although there is a danger that test results will be misleading. It is most likely that in terms of the goals set up for the program, some tests would not be adequate measures of the kinds of things which the program considered important. Essentially, then, it is most important to consider the goals of the program in selecting the test to be used.

It would seem from an examination of the literature that a variety of achievement tests are used to evaluate personalized reading programs. The Gates Reading Test, the California Reading Test, the SRA Reading Test, the Metropolitan Achievement Test, and the Iowa Tests are commonly used. The results of any of these achievement tests could be used to compare the group in the personalized program with a basal class of the same grade and age, and approximately the same mental ability, to determine the advancement made by each group. Another way would be merely to measure the progress of the class as compared with test norms to determine if one year's progress was made during the year. This could not be a valid measure of the brighter student because more than a year's progress would be expected normally, while less than a year's progress would be expected from the below average group. Such a comparison would provide the teacher with information as to the success of the program in teaching what the test assumed was important in the skills program. Such test results might also be compared with the progress the children had made in a previous year under the basal program. In this manner the either above average or below average learning rate of the class could partially be accounted for.

Vite used the Gates Primary Reading Test and stated that under the new program all of the children were at their chronological age or above in reading ability.[2] Olson reported on a study by Dunklin at Columbia University in 1940 where experimental groups which used personalized methods were set up. At the end of seven months, the experimental group was almost half a grade ahead of the control group.[3] In a study in 1948, Jones reported that those children who were taught at their individual level were able to achieve greater amount of growth than comparable pupils taught as a group. They were superior in arithmetic, spelling, and total achievement, as well as in reading.[4]

More recent test research in the field of personalized reading reveals the following:

A three-year study of 359 pupils in first grade, conducted by Gerald Gleason and called, "Lakeshore Curriculum Study Council Individualized Reading Study," paired 28 classrooms. One group taught the personalized approach and the other taught the basal approach. The pupils remained in the same classes for the entire three years but had different teachers each year. Results showed that the pupils in the individualized group scored significantly higher than did the basal group on eight of 13 standardized achievement tests. It found a greater range of scores in the basal group and no significant differences in oral reading or attitudes. It found that parents of pupils in individualized reading had more positive attitudes toward their children's reading program than did parents of basal group pupils.[5]

Elizabeth Teigland, in a study called "Experimental Study in Individualized and Basal Reader Approaches to Teaching Reading in Grades One and Two," found that when the California Reading Test was administered at the end of the second grade, the individualized reading group had significantly higher scores on comprehension than did the basal group. The vocabulary scores favored the individualized group, but were not significant. No significant differences were found in atittude toward reading according to the San Diego County Inventory of Reading Attitudes. Girls made significantly higher scores than boys on comprehension, vocabulary, and attitudes toward reading.

The quantity, variety and difficulty of books read overwhelmingly favored the individualized approach.[6]

Rodney Johnson, in a study called "A Three Year Longitudinal Study Comparing Individualized and Basal Reading Programs at the Primary Level," found the children in individualized reading programs showed significantly better reading achievement than children in basal reading programs.[7]

Mary Huser, in a three month study comparing individualized reading with basal reading in 12 intermediate classrooms, found the following:

A. The results in achievement for the experimental group using an individualized method of reading were not significantly better than when the student were taught by the traditional textbook method. There were differences that favored the individualized group, but not significant at the 10 percent level.

B. When separated into groups according to classes, the sixth grade did significantly better in reading achievement when taught by the individualized method.

C. The intermediate grade students had a more favorable attitude toward reading when taught individually than when taught in groups.

D. The overall summary of the study indicated that attitudes formed during the intermediate grades are as important, perhaps more so, to the future success and self-image of the preadolescent child as reading achievement.[8]

Bruce Appleby, in a study called "Individualized Reading in the Literature Program," found that after one year of such a course at the Keokuk, Iowa Senior High School, 85 percent of the incoming seniors requested to take it. With this impetus, a study was undertaken to determine what differences exist between students who take individualized reading and those who do not. Test seven of the ITED and the Inventory of Satisfactions Found in Reading Fiction were administered to students in an individualized reading program, to students who wanted the program but weren't taking it, and to students in a required literature course. In the inventory category of relaxation, escape, and associational values, the individualized reading group was favored, but the differences were not statistically significant. In the category of information gained from fiction, the differences favored the individualized reading group and was significant at the .01 level. Results favorable to individualized reading were also significant in the area of self-development, as well as from the ITED. He concluded that when used in conjunction with other methods of teaching literature, individualized reading appears to increase students' enjoyment of, feeling for and understanding of literature.[9]

Amount and Variety of Reading Material

The second method of evaluation which is objective enough as one measure but which must not be used alone as the criterion for determining the success of the program, is the number of books read by the children. Since the personalized program has as its very basic principle the presentation of and stimulation to read a large number of books, the teacher who feels that the program is a success merely because her pupils have read more books is operating under a false assumption. Quantity alone is not the measure of success, although it is hoped that mere number of books read will be some indication of ability to read and interest in reading.

Sperber reports that in the third grade experimental group receiving personalized instruction each child had read an average of 33 books. In the ten other classes with the basal reading program, each child had read an average of slightly less than six books.[10] This type of report is common to almost every report on personalized programs.

In addition to the number of books read, another evaluating factor might well be the diversity of the reading of the pupils. It is not at all unusual for elementary school children to become interested in one particular subject, such as dogs, horses, or science, and then want to read only in this area. The teacher in the individualized program should have the development of new reading interests as one of her goals.

An interesting evaluative technique is noted by Vite. She refers to the usual dropoff in reading ability over the summer months. Vite feels that children who have the personalized program do not lose ground over the summer months, probably because they have been more highly motivated to read for pleasure and have received guidance in knowing how to select material for themselves.[11]

Attitude

A third method of evaluation deals with attitudes. Attitudes must be measured informally, but with care. Questionnaires can be prepared which measure the attitudes of children toward the program, their parents' attitudes, and even the attitudes of teachers.

In addition to the attitudes of the children toward the program, their attitudes toward reading itself is a measurable factor. Sperber developed a reading attitude inventory consisting of 12 questions, each with three answer choices describing activities nine-year-old children engage in. One of the three choices dealt with some aspect of reading. Those in the personalized program.

chose more of the activities involving reading than did the children who had been in the basal reading program.[12]

Greenman and Katilin, after studying an experimental personalized reading program, reported better than average test gains, wider range of reading interest, no labeling of students' abilities, increase in comprehension ability, enjoyment of reading by all children, and greater retention of skills and vocabulary.[13] Such an enthusiastic report can hardly be overlooked.

The intangibles which indicate success of the program are difficult to measure. Perhaps they can only be noted, but they, too, have great value, perhaps far more than the mere tangible results of standardized tests. Parkin states this exceedingly well: "Then there are certain gains she (the teacher) cannot help observing: freedom of choice and the joy that accompanies it; release from the tethering gait of the group; release from the stigma of the group label; a relaxed attitude toward reading; the pleasure of making reading a live, dynamic activity; more time for reading for the purposes that reading can serve; a change of emphasis from competition with the group to competition with one's self."[14]

There has been little research, other than "action research," on the personalized reading program. As more people become aware of what such a program actually is, more research will be forthcoming. Veatch says, "While teachers using an individualized approach are increasingly reporting highly significant gains in achievement along with startling changes in attitude toward the instructional reading program, it is undeniable that well-grounded research is needed. The next few years will undoubtedly see more and more attention to the evaluation of (personalized) individualized reading programs."[15]

Personalized Reading Instruction: A Program That Works

The continuing interest in personalized reading is evidenced by the increasing number of research studies being undertaken in the field. Too often, however, the value of these experiments is limited by the short duration of the studies. Following is a report of a six year longitudinal study of personalized reading at J. Nelson Kelly Elementary School in Grand Forks, North Dakota. Although the design is perhaps limited, the data is viewed from many perspectives so as to ascertain honestly the growth of children who participated in the program.

Achievement Data

Because the Iowa Test of Basic Skills was the test used by the district, all achievement data is based upon this test. Test results are reported for each school year from 1966 to 1972, with the exception of school years 1967-1968 and 1968-1969. Tests were given during those years, but the data were not tabulated. (All tests were administered in September.)

Because a comparison was made between basal reading and personalized reading during school year 1969-1970, every effort was made to keep the samples pure. (That is not difficult with basal reading because they rarely used anything else. It is more difficult with personalized reading because they were likely not to have children in the program 100 percent of the time.) Each teacher was asked to make the best guess possible as to how much of a pupil's time was spent in personalized reading. This provided assurance that the comparison was between basal reading and personalized reading, and not basal reading and a contaminated sample of personalized reading. (A contaminated sample would be children who might have spent just as much time in basal reading as they did personalized reading.)

An effort was also made to evaluate only those children who had spent considerable time in personalized reading. It didn't seem appropriate to evaluate a group of children on personalized reading if many of them had transferred from schools not using the method. The data reported is always a pure sample of children who have not only spent the greatest part of their reading time in personalized reading, but who have been exposed to it over a period of several years. For that reason, the data becomes more meaningful each year it is reported. Following is a summary of the varoius research data kept during those years:

A. *School Year 1966-1967*

The data presented for this year can be considered the baseline achievement data. The group was made up of 35 children with a mean I.Q. of 116. They came to the school when it opened in the fall of 1966 as Intermediate Six students, and within three weeks were given the Iowa Test of Basic Skills. Therefore, all of their achievement is the result of instruction in other schools. It can also be assumed that this group had spent 100 percent of their time in basal readers. Their scores are as follows:

Year	Vocabulary	Reading Comprehension	Language Skills	Study Skills	Comp.
1966-1967	7.30	7.20	7.40	7.20	7.17

Figure (8-1)

B. No data was tabulated for school years 1967-1968 and 1968-1969.

C. *School Year 1969-1970*

During the school year 1969-1970 the principal was director of an intern principal project which made him principal of four schools. This gave him data that would not otherwise have been available. He selected a control group of 22 Intermediate Six students from one of the schools with a mean I.Q. of 116. The experimental group was a group of 22 Intermediate Six students from J. Nelson Kelly Elementary School with a mean I.Q. of 116. The control group spent 100 percent of their time in basal reading while the experimental group spent about 80 percent of their time in personalized reading and 20 percent of their time in basal reading. Upon administration of an attitude scale called "Hansen Self-Commitment to Independent Reading Scale," it was found that 50 percent of the control group showed commitment to reading, while 80 percent of the experimental group showed commitment. It was concluded that, according to this scale, commitment can be taught without loss of achievement. The scores for each group are as follows:

	Year	Vocabulary	Reading Comprehension	Comp.
Control	1969-1970	7.40	6.90	6.90
Experimental	1969-1970	7.40	7.00	7.00

Figure (8-2)

D. *School Year 1970-1971*

The data for school year 1970-1971 are meaningful because the amount of time spent in basal reading decreased to 12 percent of the child's reading time and the sample included a group of 24 Intermediate Six students, all of whom had been in the school and personalized reading for five years. The achievement data remained constant when compared to the baseline group of 1966-1967. (The mean I.Q. dropped three points, which is not significant.) The achievement are as follows:

Year	Vocabulary	Reading Comprehension	Language Skills	Study Skills	Comp.
1970-1971	7.30	7.10	7.00	7.20	7.00

Figure (8-3)

E. *School Year 1971-1972*

This sample includes a group of 29 Intermediate Six students, all of whom had spent six years in the school and approximately 90 percent of their time in personalized reading. There is a decrease in achievement from previous groups. This can be explained by a rather dramatic decrease in mean I.Q. from the baseline group of school year 1966-1967 (116) to school year 1971-1972 (106.7). It has been suggested that this decrease resulted from a rather significant change in the make-up of the school community during these years. The achievement data for school year 1971-1972 are as follows:

Year	Vocabulary	Reading Comprehension	Language Skills	Study Skills	Comp.
1971-1972	6.70	6.30	6.60	6.50	6.40

Figure (8-4)

F. *Data Showing Growth*

Another way to look at the achievement data is to take a group like the 29 students who were in Intermediate Six in school year 1971-1972 and make a growth chart from the time they were in Primary Three until Intermediate Six. This was done, as was a growth chart of the whole class. The latter has less meaning because it contains a very transient sample. In both cases it was found that normal growth took place. (10 months per year)

G. *Comparison of the Iowa Test of Basic Skills with Similar Schools*

Still another way of looking at achievement data is to summarize scores of several groups of students who entered the junior high school from a number of elementary schools, all of whom took the Iowa test of Basic Skills in the fall, and make a comparison. The following chart rather dramatically shows that a given group of seventh graders, all of whom had been in personalized reading for six years, with approximately the same mean I.Q. scored better than those students who had been exposed almost totally to basal reading. The chart is as follows on page 178.

H. *Individual Inventories*

Individual inventories are another way to make an assumption about how well children are reading and what kind of growth is taking place. During school year 1969-1970, Jeanette Ferrie, an Intermediate Four

No.	I.Q.	Sample	Year	Vocab.	Read. Comp.	Spell.	Lang.	Work Study	Comp.
204	111.4	Seventh Graders from Four Schools	1971-1972	8.00	7.70	7.70	7.70	7.90	7.70
60	112.2	Students from J.N. Kelly School	1971-1972	8.00	7.60	7.80	7.60	7.70	7.50
24	113.0	Students From J.N. Kelly, All of Whom Had Been in Personalized Reading Most of Their School Life	1971-1972	8.40	8.00	8.35	8.00	8.00	7.90

Figure (8-5)

teacher at J. Nelson Kelly Elementary School, did a Master's thesis on the individual conference in personalized reading. She used the Silveroli Reading Inventory as one instrument to determine reading growth. She administered the inventory to her class in September and post-tested in April. She found that 22 out of 26 children showed a year's growth or more. Four showed no gain. Of the total, eight either pre-tested at sixth level or post-tested past Intermediate Six. This instrument does not show growth above Intermediate Six level. In school year 1971-1972 a class of 59 Intermediate Four children were given the Silveroli in the fall and again in the spring. The mean growth for that group increased from 4.00 in the fall testing to 5.30 in the spring testing. All of these children spent at least 80 percent of their time in personalized reading.

I. *Teacher Privilege from the City Library*

Schools which utilize personalized reading must pay scrupulous attention to a steady flow of reading materials coming into the school. Besides the normal sources of books, the central library and the bookmobile, the Grand Forks school system is fortunate to have a cooperative relationship with the city library. The library allows teachers to check out up to 50 books per month. The books are transported both ways by the buildings and grounds department of the school district so that there is no inconvenience to the teacher. Upon careful examination of teacher privilege checkout from school year 1966-1967 to school year 1971-1972, together with reported circulation figures from the elementary libraries from 14 elementary schools during the school year 1969-1970, the following generalizations can be made:

1. The average number of books circulated in the school libraries for all elementary schools during school year 1969-1970 was 42. The average number of books circulated at J. Nelson Kelly Elementary School during that year was 53. (The school was new and had few books in the central library.)

2. There was an average of 755 books circulated in teacher privilege during school year 1969-1970 in all elementary schools, and 2,503 at J. Nelson Kelly School. The city librarian felt that because a book was in the school for one month it should be assumed that there were about three circulations per book. On that basis, an average of 2,265 books were circulated in all of the other schools, and 7,509 were circulated at J. Nelson Kelly Elementary School. The average per pupil circulation through teacher privilege was five for all of the other schools and 18.2 for J. Nelson Kelly Elementary School. When this was averaged together with the circulation in the central libraries for school year 1969-1970, the city-wide average circulation per child was 47 and 71.2 for J. Nelson Kelly Elementary School.

3. The city-wide average of checkout of books through teacher privilege for six years from school year 1966-1967 to school year 1971-1972 was 3,934. The total number checked out by the J. Nelson Kelly staff during that time was 13,038.

There seems to be little doubt that teachers of personalized reading use resources associated with reading significantly more than do teachers in basal programs. And it must be kept in mind that the averages indicated in this study include many teachers who enthusiastically support personalized reading and are utilizing resources equally well.

J. *Number of Books Read*

Although a comparison of numbers of books read with schools utilizing the basal reading approach was not available during this study, data were kept at J. Nelson Kelly Elementary School during the entire six years. During school year 1971-1972, 198 students in Intermediate Four, Five, and Six read a total of 7,475 books for an average of over 37 books per child. Every other year included in the study averaged from a low of 27 books per child to a high of 40 books per child.

K. *Circulation Comparisons of Elementary, Junior High, and High School*

It has often been stated that the golden age of reading is age 12; never do we read more than at 12 years of age. This seems to be borne out in the following data comparing circulation at all levels during school year 1969-1970.

Level	Total Volumes	Number of Schools	Enrollment	Average Circulation
Elementary	283,711	14	6,764	42
Junior High	38,824	3	2,360	16.5
Senior High	40,050	2	2,003	20

Figure (8-6)

Measuring Reading Attitudes

The greatest contribution which the personalized reading program makes is the attitude of the children toward reading. By being introduced to children's literature from the very beginning so they understand that the goal of reading instruction is to read, children learn to enjoy reading. It is not necessary to hope that children will transfer, somewhere at junior high level, the skills they have learned in the basal reader into the reading process itself. Under the personalized method, the reading process itself is stressed from the beginning.

If attitudes are important, can they be measured? How reliable are the present instruments? Do children exhibit behavior in the classroom and outside the classroom that reflects their attitude toward reading?

The most obvious means of determining commitment for reading is, of course, from observation. The personalized reading allows the teacher time with each child individually in the reading program so that she knows each child better. It would not be out of order for the teacher to ask the child about the things which he likes to do. Observing the child during the rest of the school day and after school also serves as a clue to his degree of commitment to reading. No formal instrument will measure as effectively as the teacher's observation.

To confirm teacher observation it is well to fashion some sort of informal instrument for determining attitudes towards reading. One common instrument is the incomplete sentence method. Incomplete sentences such as "Reading is ____ ; I'd rather read than ____ ; I like to read about ____ ; When I read aloud ____ ; Reading class is ____ ," are all good indications of a child's attitude toward reading. Dr. Lyman Hunt has developed an informal attitude inventory called "How I feel About Reading" that could also be used.[16] Dr. Paul Witty's "Witty's Interest Inventory" is another way of determining not only attitudes about reading but also things that relate to the whole life of the child.[17]

The advantage of formal instruments is that they are more specific in their measurements and allow the evaluator to determine growth in reading attitudes. The three instruments described herein utilize three methods of scoring which allow elementary children of all ages and their teachers to become involved in the measuring of attitudes.

A Scale of Reading Attitude Based on Behavior

This scale was developed by C. Glennon Rowell and is based upon three premises: (1) attitude is reflected in behavior; (2) this behavior can be recorded by an observer who uses a properly designed instrument; (3) an instrument used by an observer to measure attitude toward reading should provide the observer with an opportunity to check one of several different degrees of reactions to reading situations.[18] The reading attitude scale consists of 16 weighted items. Items one through six define various reading situations as they would take place in reading classes; items seven through 13 represent the area of reading for pleasure; and the last three items on the attitude scale relate to how children feel about reading in the content areas. As each item is observed, the teacher or some other observer scores the item. Careful considerations must be given to accurate observations. For instance, if the observer scored item ten high upon seeing the child go to the library one time, a gross error would have been made. This instrument should be used only when the observer knows the children involved and has observed them many times in many kinds of situations, as seen in Figure (8-7).

A Scale of Reading Attitude Based on Behavior[19]

Name of Student _____ Grade _____ Date ____	
School _____ Observer _____	
Directions: Check the most appropriate of the five blanks by each item below. Only one blank by each item should be circled.	

	Always Occurs	Often Occurs	Occasionally Occurs	Seldom Occurs	Never Occurs
1. The student exhibits a strong desire to come to the reading circle or to have reading instruction take place.	____	____	____	____	____
2. The student is enthusiastic and interested in participating once he comes to the reading circle or the reading class begins.	____	____	____	____	____

	Always Occurs	Often Occurs	Occasionally Occurs	Seldom Occurs	Never Occurs
3. The student asks permission or raises his hand to read orally.	____	____	____	____	____
4. When called upon to read orally the student eagerly does so.	____	____	____	____	____
5. The student very willingly answers a question asked him in the reading class.	____	____	____	____	____
6. Contributions in the way of voluntary discussions are made by the student in the reading class.	____	____	____	____	____
7. The student expresses a desire to be read to by you or someone else, and he attentively listens while this is taking place.	____	____	____	____	____
8. The student makes an effort to read printed materials on bulletin board, charts, or other displays having writing on them.	____	____	____	____	____
9. The student elects to read a book when the class has permission to choose a "free-time" activity.	____	____	____	____	____
10. The student expresses genuine interest in going to the school's library.	____	____	____	____	____
11. The student discusses with you (the teacher) or members of the class those items he has read from the newspaper, magazines, or similar materials.	____	____	____	____	____
12. The student voluntarily and enthusiastically discusses with others the book he has read or is reading.	____	____	____	____	____

	Always Occurs	Often Occurs	Occasionally Occurs	Seldom Occurs	Never Occurs
13. The student listens attentively while other students share their reading experiences with the group.					
14. The student expresses eagerness to read printed materials in the content areas.					
15. The student goes beyond the textbook or usual reading assignment in searching for other materials to read.					
16. The student contributes to group discussions that are based on reading assignments made in the content areas.[19]					

Reprinted with permission of C. Glennon Rowell and the International Reading Association. ("A Scale of Reading Based on Behavior," *The Reading Teacher*, February 1972, p. 444.)

Figure (8-7)

Determining Attitudes in Primary

Reading attitude inventories, although presently used by many intermediate teachers, are not in wide use at the primary level. Part of the reason for this is that there aren't many good examples of inventories that are appropriate to use with small children. Annelle Powell, Assistant Professor at the University of Virginia, has made a significant contribution in this area through her development of the Primary Reading Attitude Index.

The Primary Reading Attitude Index is based upon five different areas: (1) reading and the school library; (2) reading and the public library; (3) reading at school; (4) reading at home; and (5) personal and social aspects of reading.[20] The index contains 32 items in story form printed on five different colors of paper in the student's booklet. The question is read, and the child is asked to circle one of three faces representing happiness, sadness, and ambivalence. In all cases the child is asked to state how he feels. Although this index is not highly conducive to individual diagnosis, it does lend itself well to measuring overall changes in attitude of a group toward reading. The questions asked in this inventory are as follows:

Sample Item: You are playing. Someone takes away your toy. Circle the face which shows how you feel.

Sample Item: You are playing outside with a friend. Your mother calls you in to lunch. Circle the face which shows how you feel.

1. You are sitting at home. You are thinking about what to do. You take out a book to read. Circle the face which shows how you feel.

2. There's a lot more time left in reading class. The teacher says that you may do more pages in your reading workbook. Circle the face which shows how you feel.

3. You have time to read before you go to sleep. You choose a book to read or look at. Circle the face which shows how you feel.

4. You are playing outside. You go in the house to read or look at a book. Circle the face which shows how you feel.

5. The school library has just got a lot of new books. Circle the face which shows how you feel.

6. Your father is reading the newspaper. He lets you look at some of it. Circle the face which shows how you feel.

7. Your teacher is reading a poem to the class. Circle the face which shows how you feel.

8. Tomorrow the class will have more time for reading. You will do more work in the reading workbook. Circle the face which shows how you feel.

9. You have books to read at home. Circle the face which shows how you feel.

10. You have heard or read a story. You draw a picture about that story. Circle the face which shows how you feel.

11. Your class is having sharing time. You tell about a book you have read or heard read aloud. Circle the face which shows how you feel.

12. You are playing "make believe." You make believe you are someone from a story you have read or heard read aloud. Circle the face that shows how you feel.

13. You are at home having dinner. Your parents ask you if you have read or heard a good story. Circle the face which shows how you feel.

14. You have written a story about yourself. The teacher lets you read it to the class. Circle the face which shows how you feel.

15. You're going to the school library to hear a story. Circle the face which shows how you feel.

16. There's a lot more time left in reading class. The teacher says that you can read more in your reading book. Circle the face which shows how you feel.

17. You can either listen to someone read a story or see the story on television. You listen to someone read the story. Circle the face which shows how you feel.

18. Your mother goes shopping. She buys you a book. Circle the face which shows how you feel.

19. You and your friends are going to do something together. You decide to look at a book. Circle the face which shows how you feel.

20. The class is doing arithmetic (mathematics). It is time to listen to a story. Circle the face which shows how you feel.

21. Tomorrow the class will have more time for reading. You will be able to look at any books in the room. Circle the face which shows how you feel.

22. You are eating breakfast. You read the cereal box. Circle the face which shows how you feel.

23. You have learned a poem. You say it to the class. Circle the face which shows how you feel.

24. Tomorrow the class will have more time for reading. You will read more in your reading book. Circle the face which shows how you feel.

25. You see some of your friends. You tell them about a book you have read or heard read aloud. Circle the face which shows how you feel.

26. You are looking at a magazine. Circle the face which shows how you feel.

27. You are looking at pictures in a catalogue. Circle the face which shows how you feel.

28. You have grown up. You read a lot. Circle the face which shows how you feel.

29. You are going to the public library. Someone reads a story. Circle the face which shows how you feel.

30. You have time to do what you want to do. You make up a poem. Circle the face which shows how you feel.

31. Your class is doing reading and arithmetic (mathematics). You are doing your reading. Circle the face which shows how you feel.

32. You are trying to make a rhyme. Circle the face which shows how you feel.[21]*

Determining Attitudes in Intermediate

Most attitude inventories used above Primary Three are constructed in such a way that the child is asked to read an item and check his response. One such instrument developed by Dr. Harlan Hansen is called "The Hansen Self-Commitment to Independent Reading Scale."—Figure (8-8). The scale was built on the premise that a reading achievement test score does not necessarily account for the observed differences in children's involvement in and enjoyment of independent reading.[22] It asks the child to check "always," "usually," "seldom," and "never" on 18 items, all of which are paired. A score of 54 or higher on the scale indicates a positive self-commitment to reading while a score of 53 or lower indicates a negative self-commitment. This is arrived at by assigning values of 4 (always), 3 (usually), 2 (seldom), and 1 (never), and multiplying the number of items by the minimum positive score (3). The validity is .76, the reliability is .95 and the standard error is 2.64. The instrument is not intended to be used below Intermediate Four. (See Figure (8-8) on page 187.)

Evaluating Summer Programs

The typical summer reading program identifies all of the children who need remedial attention and gives them an intensive experience in reading skills. Because of this emphasis in the past, most children invited into such a program come knowing they have failed and have a very difficult time using this experience to build a positive self-image or to improve their reading skills.

In the spring of 1970, the North Dakota Department of Public Instruction made Title I funds available for summer programs. The Grand Forks Public and Parochial Schools Applied for $14,000 of these funds and implemented a program called, "Lifetime Readers Project."

The first thing to be done was to find a sample of children for the project. Because the project was centered around lifetime commitment to reading and only incidently dealt with skill development in other areas, the Hansen Self-

---

*Reprinted by permission of Annelle Powell, "Primary Reading Attitude Index" (Athens, Georgia: University of Georgia, 1971).

(Note: Annelle Powell has also developed an Intermediate Reading Attitude Index. Information can be obtained by writing directly to her.)

HANSEN SELF COMMITMENT TO INDEPENDENT READING SCALE

Date _____

School _____

Always	Usually	Seldom	Never	Statement
4	3	2	1	1. I like to read during my free time.
1	2	3	4	2. I would rather do almost anything but read.
4	3	2	1	3. I enjoy the characters and ideas in books.
1	2	3	4	4. I think reading is boring.
4	3	2	1	5. I wish I had more time for reading.
1	2	3	4	6. I only read when someone forces me to read.
4	3	2	1	7. Many books appeal to me.
1	2	3	4	8. Life is just as much fun without having to read.
4	3	2	1	9. I find myself wanting to read when I should be doing other things.
1	2	3	4	10. I do not like to read during my free time.
4	3	2	1	11. I like to read better than anything else I do.
1	2	3	4	12. My mind wanders from the book when I try to read.
4	3	2	1	13. Reading is fun for me.
1	2	3	4	14. If I had more time I would rather do anything but read.
4	3	2	1	15. I spend a lot of my spare time reading.
4	3	2	1	16. Life is fun because of books and reading.
1	2	3	4	17. I don't like to read because there are only a few good books.
1	2	3	4	18. It is difficult for me to get interested in a book.[23]

Figure (8-8)

Hansen, Harlan S., "Hansen Self Commitment to Independent Reading Scale" (Minneapolis, Minnesota, University of Minnesota, 1967).

Commitment to Independent Reading Scale was used to ascertain who among the sample of several hundred intermediate children in Title I schools showed lack of reading commitment. After all pretesting was completed and the sample determined, much time was spent with the children assuring them that this program would be exciting. Many of them candidly said, "If summer school is going to be like the ones I have gone to before, I want no part of it." Of course, they were assured that the program would be different.

The program centered around the following: (1) each child would select his own reading material from a rich supply of books, both paperback and hard cover, newspapers and magazines; (2) he would read them at his own pace; (3) this would be followed by an individual conference with the teacher; (4) he then could do a project on his book, and (5) he could work at one of a number of centers of interest (cooking, drama, music, art, etc.). Upon completion of this cycle, the book would be stamped, "This book is the private property of . . ." and given to the child to begin developing his own private library. The schedule of daily activities is a detailed example of how a day might spent. (See Figure (8-9) on page 189.)

The program had other interesting components. Many varied field trips were taken all over the area. The room was set up in a living room fashion where strict attention was given to developing a setting for maximum comfort. Great advantage was taken of the summer weather in that many class activities were held outside. In fact, the highlight of the summer was when all school sites held a "sharing fair" in the park. Snacks and Kool-Aid were provided in each area each day, and all attention was focused upon making the reading experience a pleasurable one.

The project objectives were based upon pretest and post-test data from the "Hansen Self Commitment to Independent Reading Scale" and in-service that was given to all project staff both before and during the project. Because the intent of the project was to impact all intermediate teachers in Title I schools, an intensive in-service program was held in the fall, prior to the new school year. The second summer evaluation also included achievement test data.

Surveys of children, parents, staff members and administrators indicated that the program was very successful. The following are considered the most positive aspects of summer programs such as the one described:

A.   Thousands of paperback books and individualized reading kits from Scholastic were brought into all Title I schools. Even though many books were given away, each school was left with an ample supply of books to continue the program.

B.   Test data clearly showed significant improvement in commitment from pre-test to post-test, according to the Hansen Self Commitment to Independent Reading Scale.

SAMPLE SCHEDULE OF DAILY ACTIVITIES

Time	Activity
8:00 a.m.—9:00 a.m.	Team Planning at Daily Activities. Team Leader presides. (sharing of daily logs, reports of successful activities, presenting of plans which require arrangements prior to activity)
9:00 a.m.—10:00 a.m.	Children arrive. All children and staff members take part in SR. (Silent Reading) Children read until they read themselves out. Conferences begin.
10:00 a.m.—11:00 a.m.	Book-Sharing. This will be any of a number of activities carried out in the classroom before the entire group, in the Centers of Interest Room, or in the neighborhood of the target school or any of the other target centers.
11:00 a.m.—12:00 a.m.	Centers of Interest Rooms. Although various centers of interest may result depending upon the direction reading takes, it is most likely that there will be a music center, art center, cooking center, drama center and writing center.
12:00 p.m.—1:00 p.m.	Noon Break
1:00 p.m.—2:00 p.m.	Unscheduled time. This time can be used to finish up anything from the morning activities. Some children may come back to school and read. Others may work in one of the centers of interest on a book sharing project or some other creative endeavor.
2:00 p.m.—	Off Campus Activities. These will begin anytime during the afternoon. Sometimes they will be a field trip with the entire group and other times a small group of children participating in some particular activity.[24]

Note: It should be noted that this is a sample schedule and not meant to be followed each day. It is planned that there will be enough flexibility in this program to allow for any activity to take place at any time during the day.

Figure (8-9)

C. It was conclusively shown that children read more when they conferenced with their teacher on a regular basis. The schools which recorded the highest number of conferences had the greatest number of books read.

D. As the number of books increased, so did commitment for lifetime reading (according to the Hansen Scale).

E. Schools which could not have been impacted in any other way suddenly became hostels of personalized reading.

F. This project found a way to in-service teachers in the area of personalized reading in a way that was acceptable to all concerned.

G. Individual libraries began to be developed in homes, and parents seemed to take a more active interest in their child's reading.

H. Children, many of them for the first time, developed positive attitudes about attending summer school.

Summary

The questions surrounding evaluation of reading will forever be the subject of much debate and discussion, both within and outside of the profession. Because knowing how to read and using the skill is so inherently tied both to one's material success and to one's image of self, it becomes crucial that all people develop the skill to the very best of their ability.

The key to evaluation of reading programs is to first know what kind of an end product is desired. If the concern is totally centered around "how" to read, one set of evaluative measures will be used. If on the other hand, there is some concern about lifetime commitment to reading, there will be stress upon measures that attempt to evaluate not only achievement data, but also data which deals with attitudes toward reading.

It is well-known that it is just as easy to find research studies unfavorable to personalized reading as it is to find favorable ones. However, research of the past ten years does seem to verify what has been thought for a long time: An enthusiastic teacher will make personalized reading work as well or better than other kinds of reading programs insofar as skill development is concerned, and will do a far better job of building favorable attitudes toward reading.

FOOTNOTES

[1]Paul Witty, *Reading and Modern Education* (Boston, Massachusetts: D.C. Heath and Company, 1949).

[2]Irene Vite, "A Primary Teacher's Experience," Chapter Two, *Individualizing Reading Practices*, Alice Meil, ed., No. 14, Practical Suggestions for Teaching (New

York, New York: Bureau of Publications, Teachers College, Columbia University), p. 42.

[3]Willard C. Olson, *Child Development* (Boston, Massachusetts: D.C. Heath and Company, 1949), p. 139.

[4]Daisy M. Jones, "An Experiment in Adaption to Individual Difference," *Journal of Education Psychology*, Vol. 39, (March 1948), pp. 257-272.

[5]Gerald T. Gleason, "Lakeshore Curriculum Study Council Individualized Reading—A Three Year Study," May 1970. (ERIC Ed. 052906)

[6]Elizabeth A. Teigland, "An Experimental Study of Individualized and Basal Reader Approaches to Teaching Reading in Grades One and Two" (New York, New York: Paper presented at the conference of the American Educational Research Association, February 4-7, 1971.) (ERIC Ed. 047901)

[7]Rodney Johnson, "A Three Year Longitudinal Study Comparing Individualized and Basal Reading Programs at the Primary Level," an Interm Report. (ERIC Ed. 010979)

[8]Mary K. Huser, "Reading and More Reading," *Elementary English*, April 1967, pp. 381-382.

[9]Bruce C. Appleby, "Individualized Reading in the Literature Program" (ERIC Ed. 018411)

[10]Robert Sperber, "An Individualized Reading Program in a Third Grade," Chapter Three, *Individualizing Reading Practices*, Alice Meil, ed., No. 14, Practical Suggestions for Teaching (New York, New York: Bureau of Publications, Teachers College, Columbia University), pp. 45-51.

[11]Irene Vite, "A Primary Teacher's Experience," p. 41.

[12]Sperber, "An Individualized Reading Program in a Third Grade," p. 51.

[13]Ruth Greenman and Sheran Katilin, "Individualized Reading in Third and Fourth Grades," *Elementary English*, Vol. 36, April 1959, pp. 234-237.

[14]Phyliss B. Parkin, "An Individual Program of Reading," *Educational Leadership*, Vol. 14, October 1956, pp. 37-38.

[15]Jeannette Veatch, "Children's Interest and Individual Reading," *The Reading Teacher*, Vol. 10, No. 3, February 1957, p. 165.

[16]Lyman Hunt, "How I Feel About Reading" (Burlington, Vermont: University of Vermont, 1967).

[17]Paul Witty, "Witty Interest Inventory" (Evanston, Illinois: Northwestern University, 1948).

[18]Glennon C. Rowell, "An Attitude Scale for Reading," *The Reading Teacher*, February 1972, pp. 442-447.

[19]Rowell, "An Attitude Scale for Reading," p. 444.

[20]Annelle Powell, "Primary Reading Index" (Charlotteville, Virginia: University of Virginia, 1971).

[21]Powell, "Primary Reading Index," Student Manual.

[22]Harlan Hansen, "Hansen Self Commitment to Independent Reading Scale," (Minneapolis, Minnesota, University of Minnesota, 1967).

[23]Hansen, "Hansen Self Commitment to Independent Reading Scale."

[24]Andrew Swanson and Larry Hoiberg, *Grand Forks Lifetime Readers Project* (Grand Forks, North Dakota: Grand Forks Public Schools, 1970-1972).

chapter nine

Questions Teachers Ask About Personalized Reading Instruction

---

There are many problems confronting the teacher or school which considers shifting to personalized reading instruction. Whether or not the benefits outweigh the difficulties which must be overcome can only be answered at the local level. Any attempt to dictate that the personalized philosophy is better in all situations would only be an indication of the same degree of rigidity as that held by the proponents of other reading programs.

Within the classroom itself there are a number of implications of adopting personalized reading that must be carefully examined. Following is a delineation of the most commonly asked questions about this method.

1) Why do we need personalized reading?

Personalized reading is needed in today's classrooms because of the over-reliance by many teachers on basal readers. Although basal readers may do the job of teaching children how to read, they do little to cultivate a love for reading. Personalized reading has the potential not only to teach children how to read as well as in any other program, but also to teach children to love reading and use it as a lifelong skill.

2) Is personalized reading for the master teacher only?

No. Any teacher can utilize personalized reading if the determination and enthusiasm is present. It has been used successfully by both new and experienced classroom teachers, as well as student teachers. With training, student tutors and parent aides perform well in certain aspects of the program. One of the marvelous aspects of this program is that it has the potential to make a master teacher out of a very average teacher. The nature of the program forces the teacher to learn more about children's books than ever thought possible, work intensively with children on a one-to-one basis, as well as learn the skill sequence in a much more detailed way.

3) Can one teacher do this alone?

No teacher should ever function alone. If preparation for an adult world is one of the objectives of schooling, no child should interact only with his teacher. University students and other children in the school should be utilized. Parents should be invited to participate. Drafting the help of these resource people is the only solution that will immediately let the boys and girls in classrooms have the teacher-pupil ratio that decent education demands.

4) Can one teacher on a staff utilize personalized reading while all others are utilizing a basal approach?

Whenever implementing any curricular change it is well to have more than one teacher involved because of the mutual sharing that takes place and because of the support teachers need while striking out into the unknown. However, if enthusiasm for the method is high, and support from parents and supervisors is present, teachers should not postpone or cancel implementation.

5) What effect will personalized reading instruction have upon the teacher?

The implications of the personalized program's effect on the teacher's ability to teach reading are perhaps of greatest importance. For a long time educational researchers have warned of the dangers of implementing curricular changes without considering the effects upon the teacher. To implement a program without proper background will almost always cause the teacher to give complete attention to details and forget about teaching the underlying principles. This makes it imperative that teachers have proper training before any curricular innovation. Personalized reading is no panacea. It will not make up for deficiency within the teacher's training, mental ability, or personality. It should provide a means, however, by which good teachers can do an even better job of teaching reading. There will, of course, be some children who will have difficulty in learning to read, but the personalized program provides a means by which the classroom teacher will have both the time and the materials to aid those students at their level, rather than expecting them to fit in any of several groups within the classroom.

6) How important is the teacher's attitude in this program?

More than in any other type of program, the teacher's attitude toward reading will affect the attitude of the children in the classroom. If the teacher cannot find time to read herself, then it is not likely that she will take full advantage of the individual conference and develop good attitudes toward reading. Only if the teacher herself truly appreciates literature, including adult literature, as well as children's literature, can it be expected that the child will "catch" the joy of reading.

7) What effect will personalized reading have upon the relationship between the child and his teacher?

One of the greatest arguments in favor of this philosophy is the positive relationship which it allows between the pupil and the teacher in a person-to-person relationship. There can be no question but that individual instruction provides for the greatest exchange of information between the pupil and the teacher, as well as the greatest depth of understanding and appreciation of one another's points of view. In mass education, such one-to-one relationships are frequently impossible, but in the personalized reading program, limited in time as it may be, one-to-one relationships are an essential factor of the program.

8) Can teachers become proficient enough in diagnosis to adequately ascertain the skill needs of children?

Yes. In fact, the experience of the authors has shown that teachers become more proficient in the teaching of skills when they leave the safe havens of the basal materials and dare to risk making their own diagnosis. In the beginning of the program there will be heavy reliance upon the basal materials. As time passes, the teacher will no doubt rely more heavily upon her own diagnostic skills.

9) Can I be assured that the children in my class will learn skills as well as they did in the basal program?

Most studies show that children in personalized reading score as well in achievement tests as do children in basal programs. Teachers who are highly concerned about test scores should chart data from time to time to assure themselves that skills are indeed being taught. To compare the reading levels of children in the personalized program with those in the basal reader would be misleading. The achievement tests are measuring essentially those skills which are taught in the basal reading program only, omitting the more important skills such as ability to select appropriate materials, the frequency itself with which such materials are chosen, and attitudes and interests in reading.

10) How do I group for skills?

Of course teachers will want to avoid placing children in three, or more, ability groups for long periods of time. Rather, the children should be grouped around common needs. As soon as those needs are met, the group should disband and new ones form. It should be remembered that spelling and handwriting classes are excellent places to teach word analysis skills. Children should be inspired to write much and often, for when writing is good, reading will be good. Teachers should scan writing papers and make piles showing single errors such as: (1) incomplete blends and digraphs; (2) problems of syllabication; (3) inability to spell parts of words; and (4) inability to add prefixes and suffixes, to get clues to grouping.

Jeannette Veatch says it well when she says: "Those revealed categories of needs from written work can be the topic for group teaching during the reading period. Word analysis skills should be taught mainly as spelling skills. Then the ability to hear sounds of letters, to hear syllables in words, and to hear whole words, is available to the teacher when needed during the instructional reading period. Word analysis skills are needed during reading, obviously, but they are introduced, and built in the spelling or written language part of the curriculum."[1]

11) Is a five minute conference enough to adequately diagnose strengths and weaknesses?

Personalized reading is often criticized because of the amount of time children spend in the conference. One or two five minute conferences per week, argue the critics, is not enough time to adequately diagnose the strengths and weaknesses of a child without considering the many other things that are to be accomplished in the conference. First, it must be understood that this is not the only time during the language arts period that a child interacts with his teacher. There are many opportunities for children to work with a teacher in groups. Secondly, when the typical reading class is examined, rarely does each individual child get five minutes of private time with his teacher. Insofar as word analysis skills are concerned, it has already been established that the conference, although useful for identifying skill strengths and weaknesses, is not the best time to work on them. Spelling and handwriting classes are much more appropriate times for word analysis skills.

12) Do the children continue to learn new skills after they have achieved mastery at one level?

It is not the purpose of the personalized reading program to push children through reading skills at any faster pace so they will make higher scores on reading achievement tests. In this present "craze" for being above national norms more emphasis is being placed upon getting through faster than upon quality. The personalized reading program does not provide for teaching children reading skills at the next higher level until the child reaches that level.

13) How do I determine reading level?

Finding instructional level is vital in personalized reading just as it is in any other kind of a reading program. Basal readers and other inventories are available to help with this diagnosis. Proceed with caution for instructional level is closely related to interest level. If interest is high, children will read more difficult material than indicated by an inventory.

14) Reading teachers are often criticized because they fail to see the totality of language. Can this be avoided in the personalized program?

Although it depends almost totally upon the skill of the teacher, there are some aspects of personalized reading that do provide for amalgamation of all facets of language. For instance, the teacher of personalized reading, utilizing seeking, self-selection, and pacing, will begin to develop individual vocabulary and spelling lists, utilize the child's own language to a greater extent, and get far more writing from children than in basal programs. This alone should help children see the relationship between the various aspects of language.

15) What provisions are made for transfer of learning from one particular area to another?

Again, when children seek and self-select their own reading materials, and read them at their own pace, there is ample opportunity for transfer of learning. An examination of the reading material of any given class, at any given time, will indicate tremendous divergence of subject matter. If the teacher capitalizes upon this great wealth of material, the class will be deeply involved in every subject area nearly all of the time.

16) How do I use the basal reader?

The teacher's manual is unquestionably the greatest contribution of the basal reading series. The degree of quality of the activities outlined in these manuals is not easily surpassed. It is not unlikely that even in the personalized reading program, the classroom teacher would frequently refer to the basal reading manuals of different publishing companies to understand better how to present certain skills which the children are to learn. It is also recommended that the teacher bring together at different times certain basal readers for groups of children to use when they are learning a particular skill. Of course, there would be no going from one story to another within the basal reader for that would destroy the very basis of the personalized program. If the teacher found this to be happening, she would need to understand that the routine, habit-forming pattern of the groups, with each child reading one story each day, was threatening her efforts to teach the children to love reading.

17) At what grade level should personalized reading begin?

Many factors need to be considered when answering this question. First, the readiness of the teacher to begin the program. If the teacher is enthusiastic about the approach, and has a sound knowledge of the reading skills, there is no reason why she cannot begin at any level. Second, if personalized reading implies that time which a child is independent enough to seek and self-select his own reading materials, he could be started sometime during the second year in school (Primary I). Third, if one takes the broader definition of personalized reading, that is, utilizing the child's own language in the teaching of reading, it can begin the first day he enters school. In other words, personalization of reading can take place immediately, only the form changes somewhat.

18) How do I launch the program?

Although this book describes various ways to implement personalized reading, (reading, in-service, visiting successful programs, experimenting with part of the class, etc.) it is usually best to move into the program at a speed comfortable to the reader. Plan success. If the teacher feels as though the children are being shortchanged in any way, she should analyze what is taking place. Some teachers, reticent about the skills part of personalized reading, wait until a group finishes the basal program. Others use the method with gifted readers. As teachers see the successes in this way, they feel better about a broader implementation.

19) Could you outline a process that could be followed by a very traditional teacher who works alone, with one basal reader and three groups?

Although the steps in this process could be changed somewhat, following is an example of a sequence that could be followed:

A) Use of multi-basals
B) Read stories out of sequence
C) Conference with basal stories
D) Invite others to help conference with children
E) Begin recreational reading (each child selects a book that he reads for enjoyment)
F) Utilize book-sharing
G) Implement Uninterrupted Sustained Silent Reading
H) Implement centers of interest
I) Experiment with various kinds of skills grouping
J) Begin the program with part of the class or a group which has finished the basal program
K) Implement self-management processes
L) Experiment with a record-keeping system that works best for you
M) Full implementation including: (1) seeking, self-selection, and pacing; (2) conferences; (3) need grouping; (4) self-management; (5) a record-keeping system; and, (6) independent activities

20) Can I begin the program without a background in children's literature?

Yes. One of the major problems in the teaching of reading is the teacher's lack of knowledge about children's literature. And worse still is the fact that current programs do little to increase that knowledge. Utilizing some of the suggestions found in this book such as conferencing with children, taking college classes, avid reading, and securing reviews of books commonly read by children will all help the teacher become an authority in children's literature in a few years.

21) Can children be trusted to seek and self-select their own books?

Yes.

22) Isn't it a poor economy of time to conference individually with children?

Not at all. In fact the individual conference is the high point of the entire program. Of course this is not to say that there aren't other ways to meet children. Part of the teacher's time should be spent in group conferences and groups of all kinds. In the beginning of the program the teacher will note an inordinate amount of time being used for conferences because of her lack of technique. This problem will disappear as the teacher becomes more experienced.

23) What do centers of interest have to do with reading?

For too long children have been taught reading in such an isolated manner as to never see why they are learning the skill. Centers of interest are openended experiences that give children ample opportunity to utilize the skills they are learning.

24) Is there a danger that teachers could devise a record-keeping system that is so complex and time-consuming as to destroy the program?

Yes. Teachers are advised to carefully study Chapter five on recordkeeping. Above all, keep it simple.

25) Can children be trusted to make all of the decisions they are asked to make in this program?

One of the greatest problems facing educators today is the lack of reality in the school. In fact, some critics feel the school world has so little connection with the real world that it should be changed radically. Some have even suggested "deschooling." Personalized reading, with its emphasis upon preparing children for independence in the real world, is a real step forward, not only in teaching them how to read and to love reading, but to take their place in a world where people are asked to be responsible for self.

26) We hear so much today about the child's self-image. Will that improve in this program?

The personalized reading program is likely to have a great effect upon the attitudes of children within the classroom toward one another, as well as toward themselves in relationship to others. Since a major part of the personalized reading program is the individual conference itself, this eliminates the child's attitude that he belongs to a particular reading group. It has long been known by classroom teachers that children themselves are not fooled by such labels as "bluebirds," "astronauts," or the name of the leader of the groups. The children know that such a group is either the "dumb" group, "average" group, or "smart" group, and frequently refer to it by these labels in spite of the teacher's efforts to call it something else. Not only have children known into which group they fell, but they have also been rather good judges of the group into which other children fall. Such categorization, which occurs frequently even at the primary level, creates an attitude in the children, both toward themselves and toward others, which is certainly not desirable. Furthermore, the traditional three-group type program sets as a goal, first of all, getting ahead of the other children in the group. As unlikely as the next goal may be, it does somehow hold out the idea that to be in the next higher group is desirable. No provision is made in such grouping for even bridging the gap between the two groups, however. If the child ever does succeed in reaching the level of the next higher group, that group has already moved on ahead and he is somewhere between the two and not a part of either. In the personalized program, in which the child is never a part of a reading level group for any prolonged period, his goal is not to get ahead of the other children in the group or to catch up with the next higher group. The goal is, instead, to improve his own reading for the single goal of enjoying reading better. By selecting his own material and pacing himself, the child is able to progress, not at the teacher's rate or at the rate of the other children, but at his own rate toward the final goal of successful reading and reading appreciation. The teacher attempts to develop within each child a desire to be a better reader, not for the goal of surpassing someone else, but instead to improve himself. This change in the basic goal of the program should provide for better attitudes within the classroom between the children themselves. Whether the child is slower or brighter, he will have his own place in the total reading program and need not be ashamed of that place. He should better be able to accept other children in the classroom for themselves, rather than for some artificial group into which they have been placed. He will not in any way be labeled as either a particularly good reader or a poor reader, but rather identify himself with the books which he is reading. This does not mean to imply that the rest of the children will not know which ones read better than others, but it means that the emphasis will be placed upon reading and not upon reading level. In short, self-image will be greatly improved as a result of implementing personalized reading.

27) Can this method be used with all children?

Yes. Many children, both gifted and slow, are being short-changed in traditional reading programs because of a failure to meet their needs. There is good rationale for this program to be used with all children.

28) What specific techniques could be used with a group of slow readers?

A) Exercise greater care in the selection of books.
B) Give them more concrete experiences in selecting books.
C) Utilize their own language as much as possible.
D) Make record-keeping as simple as possible for them.
E) Reassure them more often in the conference.
F) Make sure skill work is not at frustration level.
G) Have more conferences of shorter duration.
H) Use more multi-media materials.
I) Exercise care in length of material, numbers of questions to be answered, size of print, presence of illustrations, etc.
J) Do most of the word analysis skill work in spelling and writing.
K) Keep directions and assignments simple.
L) Be a good listener.

29) How will I control the children in this program?

Too many of the nation's reading teachers have their classes organized to promote control of the children. The objective of personalized reading is to so organize the classroom as to promote self-control. Chapter two, "Organizing the Classroom for Personalized Reading Instruction," should give many ideas to help the children become more responsible for self.

30) Does this program have any advantages for boys?

One only need examine the statistics of referrals to reading clinics to know that current programs are not meeting their needs. Most of the referrals to clinics are boys. And these boys are not being referred because they can't learn to read, but because they don't think they can learn to read. In other words, the image they hold of themselves is so low they don't think they will ever learn to read. It is becoming increasingly evident to the teachers who are using personalized reading that the boys are not only becoming interested in reading but are so motivated and aroused as to extend their reading far beyond their responses in other programs.

31) Can children transfer in and out of this program with a minimum of difficulty?

Always a problem to any program, but particularly to a new type of program, is the child who transfers either into or out of the program. Transferring into the personalized reading program should present little difficulty. The teacher may have to spend more time with the child in the initial periods of teaching him the pattern of the personalized program, but this should in no way impede his development of reading skills of reading interests and habits. Transferring out of the program will present some problems, but they are not thought to be any greater than those encountered in transferring from one basal series to another basal series, however. It is not unlikely that those children transferring out of the program will carry to their new classroom situation such convincing evidence of the value of the personalized program that the teacher in the new situation will be encouraged to try personalized reading.

32) How can parents be prepared for this program?

Any new program, particularly one involving the teaching of reading, will meet within every community both acceptance from some people eager for change and rejection by others who like the old system. There is no reason to think that the personalized reading program will be different in any way from that of other new programs. Since the teaching of reading is today so much in the public view, with every person considering himself an expert on how it should be done, it is not unlikely that the introduction of this method could cause some reactions. Following are some techniques that could be used to assure parents that their children will learn to read as well as in other programs:

A) Have a large group presentation on the merits of personalized reading.

B) Ask teachers to invite their parent group in to talk about the program.

C) Invite parents to participate in the implementation of the program.

D) Develop a record-keeping system that helps parents see careful attention to sequential skill development.

E) Take time at the end of the reading period to evaluate what has been done with the hope that it will be communicated with parents.

F) Keep careful records of data which show the positive aspects of the program.

G) Continue to talk up the "love for reading" aspect of the program.

H) Make reserach reports available to parents.

I) Show your interest in reading and children by: (1) taking children to the public library; (2) using the bookmobile; (3) reading both children's and adult books to them; (4) keeping the central library open after hours; and (5) operating bookstores for the convenience of parents and children.

33) Is there any evidence that this program is better than other reading programs?

Most studies that have been done in this area fail to conclusively show that any one reading program is truly superior to another. It is the teacher that makes the difference. However, few research studies examine anything but achievement data. Some studies that have been done show personalized reading to be superior to basal reading programs while others show the basal program to be superior. Still others show no significance. It is in the area of reading attitudes where personalized reading is truly superior to other reading programs. It would be the authors' contention, after considering all factors, that personalized reading is superior to other reading programs and must be at least a part of every reading program which hopes to teach children appreciation and love for reading as well as improvement of the skill itself.

34) Can this program be implemented without a central library or the services of a fully qualified librarian?

It would seem that if a school didn't have a library or librarian it would be all the more reason to implement the program. If a school has a library and a librarian, both should be an integral part of the program. If they have neither, it should not deter any teacher from beginning the program.

35) Are teacher training institutions preparing their students for this type of program?

Some colleges and universities are truly committed to personalized reading while others are not. Although trends are not apparent, the flood of commerical materials with a personalized philosophy, together with the results of basal teaching, is causing more and more college teachers to expound the personalized philosophy.

36) Is personalized reading expensive?

No. It is probably the least expensive program that will ever be implemented in any school. The program can be started with existing materials. Of course there are many exciting materials available if funds exist to purchase them.

37) Most of those responsible for reading programs are basal-oriented. Is it possible to build a lot of enthusiasm for the program and never be able to implement it?

It sure is. However, most supervisors, given enough information, and some assurance that the program will be successful, will support efforts to implement it.

38) Is it possible to get all the materials needed for this program?

It is never possible to get all the materials needed for any program. Beware of those who would deter your beginning the program because of some arbitrary guidelines they have set up. Begin with the materials that are available and search far and wide for more.

39) What sources should be read before beginning the program?

Ideas to implement personalized reading have increased substantially in the last few years. One of the best summaries can be found in Chapter 12 of Dr. Sam Duker's book, *Individualized Reading*.[2]

40) Are there commercial materials available that will help launch the program?

There are many fine commercial materials. Some are:
A) One-to-One, Prentice-Hall, Inc., Educational Book Division, New Jersey.
B) Random House Reading Program, Random House Singer School Division, 210 E. 50th St., New York, New York.
C) Invitations to Personal Reading, Scott Foresman, Glenview, Illinois.
D) Individualized Reading from Scholastic, Scholastic Book Services, 904 Sylvan Ave., Englewood Cliffs, New Jersey.
E) E & R Development Co. Individualized Reading Cards, E & R Development Co., Jacksonville, Illinois.
F) Personalized Reading Center, Xerox, Educational Division, Box 1195, Columbus, Ohio.
G) Satellite Books, Holt, Rinehart and Winston, 383 Madison Ave., New York, New York.

41) Is this method of teaching congruent with all of the discussion that is currently taking place relative to alternatives in education?

Yes. Most of the things being discussed today by the critics of education relative to more options and more humane treatment of children has been elucidated by those advocating personalized reading. With respect to alternatives in education, personalized reading is very compatible.

42) Is this method of teaching compatible with the industrial model of behavioral objectives and performance based on teaching that is currently being utilized in many reading programs?

Although there are instances in which the industrial model of education could be utilized in the personalized program, it is generally considered to be counter to the personalized philosophy.

Summary

The questions posed in this chapter and the answers educators give to them are crucial to the organization of any reading program. Changing the reading program is bound to have repercussions throughout the school, school system, and community itself. If the teacher, principal, and central administration are not prepared for the necessary adjustments of a new philosphy of teaching reading, it is doubtful whether or not it should be undertaken. If the program can be entered into both with confidence of success and clear evidence of the teacher's ability to handle adequately the personalized techniques, there is virtually no chance of failure.

FOOTNOTES

[1]Jeannette Veatch, *Individualized Reading, New Frontiers in Education*. (New York, New York: Grune and Stratton, Inc., 1966), p. 99.

[2]Sam Duker, *Individualized Reading* (Springfield, Illinois: Charles C. Thomas, Publisher, 1971), pp. 226-240.

Index